Obadiah, Jonah, and Micah

Mercy in the Middle

Salvation comes from the L*ORD.*

Jonah 2:9

Revised from material by J. M. Weidenschilling
Contributions by Robert C. Baker

CONCORDIA PUBLISHING HOUSE • SAINT LOUIS

Copyright © 2004 Concordia Publishing House
3558 S. Jefferson Ave., St. Louis, MO 63118-3968

1-800-325-3040 · www.cph.org

Revised from material by J. M. Weidenschilling

Contributions by Robert C. Baker

This publication may be available in braille, in large print, or on cassette tape for the visually impaired. Please allow 8 to 12 weeks for delivery. Write to the Library for the Blind, 7550 Watson Road, St. Louis, MO 63119-4409; call 1-888-215-2455; or visit the Web site: www.blindmission.org.

5 6 7 8 9 10 11 12 13 29 28 27 26 25 24 23

Contents

History	*Date* (B.C.)	*Obadiah, Jonah, and Micah*
Jehoram, King of Judah	**853–841**	
Jerusalem invaded by Philistines and Arabians 2 Kings 8:20–22; 2 Chronicles 21:16–17	**855–840**	Obadiah's call, 1:1 *(early view)*
	848–797	Elisha ministers in Israel
Jereboam II, King of Israel, 2 Kings 14:25	**793–753**	Jonah's call, 1:1
	760–715	Amos and Hosea minister in Israel
Kings of Judah: Jotham Ahaz Hezekiah	**750–732** **735–715** **715–686**	Micah's call, 1:1
	740–681	Isaiah ministers in Judah, Isaiah 1:1
Israel invaded by Sargon II, King of Assyria	**722**	
	629–585	Jeremiah ministers in Judah, Jeremiah 1:1–3
First deportation to Babylon	**597**	
Zedekiah	**597–587**	
Siege of Jerusalem begins (Nebuchadnezzar) 2 Kings 25:1–21; 2 Chronicles 36:11–20; Jeremiah 52:1–30	**589**	
Fall of Jerusalem Second deportation to Babylon	**587**	
	585–555	Obadiah's call, 1:1 *(late view)*

An Outline of Obadiah

Despite its small size, the Book of Obadiah contains verses that are full of meaning. Primarily directed against one of Israel's ancient foes, the Edomites, Obadiah nevertheless alludes to the inclusion of the Gentiles into God's plan of salvation. This will be accomplished through the ultimate Deliverer (v. 21) who will rule God's kingdom forever. Following the prophet's commission (introduction), Obadiah may be divided into three main sections:

I. Obadiah's Commission from the Lord (v. 1)
II. The Lord's Judgment against Edom (vv. 2–7)
  A. Her Pride (vv. 2–3)
  B. Her Coming Destruction (vv. 4–7)
III. The Coming Devastation against Edom (vv. 8–14)
  A. Her Shame (vv. 8–10)
  B. Her Crimes Against the Lord's People (vv. 11–14)
IV. The Day of the Lord (vv. 15–21)
  A. Retributive Justice (vv. 15–18)
  B. The Return of the Lord's Kingdom (vv. 19–21)

An Outline of Jonah

That the Gospel is also for the Gentiles is clearly manifested in the Book of Jonah. In Matthew 12 Jesus refers to Jonah's experience in the great fish as historical fact, serving as an Old Testament type of His death, burial, and resurrection. Out of all the Old Testament prophets, Jesus compares only Jonah unto Himself. Jonah's book can be neatly divided along directional lines, with each end of the compass serving as "markers" for his story:

I. Jonah's Westward Flight (1:1–2:10)
   A. His Commission from the Lord (1:1–3)
   B. His Experience on Ship (1:4–16)
   C. His Deliverance and Praise (1:17–2:10)
II. Jonah's Eastward Faithfulness (3:1–4:11)
   A. His Recommissioning from the Lord (3:1–3)
   B. His Proclamation to the Ninevites (3:4–10)
   C. His Anger and Nineveh's Deliverance (4:1–11)

An Outline of Micah

By the Spirit's power, Micah prophesies the exact birthplace of the promised Messiah: Bethlehem, a small town in Judah. Seeing over seven hundred years into the future, Micah declares His eternal divinity and His coming kingdom. Condemning idolatry, empty ritualism, and injustice, Micah points God's people to trust in the Lord who bestows mercy and forgiveness. Following the prophet's commission (introduction), Micah can be divided into three main sections:

I. Micah's Commission from the Lord (1:1)
II. Judgment, Promise, and Condemnation (1:2–3:12)
  A. Destruction for Samaria and Judah (1:2–16)
  B. Man's Ways and the Lord's Way (2:1–11)
  C. The Promise of a Remnant (2:12–13)
  D. Leaders and Prophets Condemned (3:1–12)
III. Zion and Her King Established (4:1–5:15)
  A. The Lord's Presence with His People (4:1–5)
  B. The Lord Restores the Lame (4:6–13)
  C. The Arrival of the King of Peace (5:1–5)
  D. The Lord Destroys Zion's Enemies (5:6–15)
IV. The Lord's Mercy Conquers Sin (6:1–7:20)
  A. The Lord's Case and Israel's Punishment (6:1–16)
  B. Reflections on Disobedience (7:1–6)
  C. Confidence in the Lord (7:7–17)
  D. A Prayer of Praise (7:18–20)

Introduction to Obadiah, Jonah, and Micah

Obadiah, Jonah, and Micah are three of the twelve prophetic books frequently referred to as "The Minor Prophets." Such a title is misleading, at best—for although their small size may hardly compare to larger prophetic works such as Isaiah, Jeremiah, and Ezekiel, the prophecies they contain continue to have major import for God's people. Written during a timespan of perhaps three hundred years, during which both the Northern and Southern Kingdoms collapsed, the little books brought a message of repentance and restoration to the people of Judah (Obadiah and Micah), and to the people of Israel (Jonah).

That message reverberates today, for the prophecies contained in these three books find ultimate fulfillment in Jesus Christ. Obadiah, the "servant of Yahweh," looks forward to the day when Israel's enemies will be judged and the Lord's kingdom will be established on Mt. Zion. The historically true story of Jonah shows God's desire to extend His grace to the Gentiles, and Jonah's experience in the great fish serves as an Old Testament type of Christ. Micah's words point specifically to God's desire to pardon and forgive through the promised Babe of Bethlehem, true God Himself. In our time these "minor" books continue to proclaim a "major" message: God offers His mercy in the middle of every circumstance. We are right with Him through faith in His Son.

Lesson 1

Obadiah: Servant of the Lord

The maxim "Big things come in small packages" accurately describes the prophecy of Obadiah. Consisting of merely 21 verses, Obadiah is the shortest book in the Old Testament. And yet, Obadiah's little prophecy has important things to say to God's people today, just as it did in Obadiah's day.

Obadiah means "servant" or "worshiper" of Yahweh, the Lord. Obadiah was called by God to prophesy to His people in the Southern Kingdom of Judah. His prophecy was directed primarily against the Edomites, Judah's ancient enemies and the descendants of Esau. Edom had been particularly cruel to Judah (see Exodus 15:15; Numbers 20:14–21; 2 Samuel 8:13–14; 2 Kings 8:20–22). As Judah's enemy, Edom's condemnation and destruction by the Lord signaled deliverance for God's people.

"Big Things" in a Small Package

The early church father Jerome (ca. A.D. 340–420) noted that, in spite of its small size, Obadiah presented quite a number of difficulties. One of these is that little is known about the author of the book. Although the name *Obadiah* is mentioned more than ten times in the Old Testament—some scholars have speculated that some of these refer to our author—there is scant evidence to confirm the writer's identity.

Another difficulty has to do with the dating of the prophecy. Earlier, traditional scholars placed Obadiah in Judah during the reign of Jehoram, king of Judah (848–841 B.C.). According to this view, Obadiah would have written his prophecy around 845 B.C. Other scholars believe that the book was written later. Paul Raabe, professor of exegetical theology at Concordia Seminary, St. Louis, has suggested between 585–555 B.C. as the time frame of Obadiah's book. This corresponds to what Luther and other reformers proposed.

Further, the first part of Obadiah looks remarkably similar to the forty-ninth chapter of Jeremiah. Biblical scholars have debated whether Obadiah was dependent upon Jeremiah for prophetic material or vice versa. Others have suggested that both prophets may have relied on a yet undiscovered third source of inspired material.

1. Compare Obadiah 1–4 to Jeremiah 49:14–16, and Obadiah 5–6 to Jeremiah 49:9–10, noting the similarities. Read Luke 1:1–4. How does Luke describe the process he undertook in writing his Gospel?

Obadiah's Vision

Verse 1 of Obadiah speaks about the prophet's *vision*. Frequently, the Old Testament uses this term to refer to God communicating to His chosen prophets. God reveals to them what He wants them to understand and proclaim to others.

2. Read the following passages, noticing how the word *vision* is used in describing divine prophetic revelation: Isaiah 1:1, Ezekiel 1:1, Micah 1:1, and Nahum 1:1. How does knowing that a prophet's message is divinely inspired help us in discussing Bible difficulties, such as the exact identity of biblical writers, the exact date of their writings, and remarkably comparable Bible passages?

3. Read Mark 12:36, 2 Timothy 3:16–17, and 2 Peter 1:16–21. How do Jesus and the apostles describe the Holy Spirit's role in writing the Scriptures, including Obadiah's little book?

A State of the Heart

Obadiah's prophecy consists primarily of three oracles of judgment addressed to Judah's enemies: verses 1–4, 5–7, and 8–15. On the "day of the LORD" God's people will have two reasons to rejoice: justice will be administered to her enemies, and the kingdom of Zion will be reestablished. The ancient struggle between Jacob and Esau—perpetuated through the actions of their descendants—would finally be over.

Edom's pride, which had manifested itself in centuries of hostility towards Israel, warranted God's judgment and condemnation. Edom's pride had deceived their hearts (v. 3). Rather than trusting in the Lord, they put their hope in their own wisdom, hoping to exalt themselves (v. 4) over others. By trusting in themselves, they showed their arrogance and conceit.

4. Read Genesis 3:1–13. How was Eve's heart (and later Adam's) deceived? Note the similarities in Obadiah 2–4 and Isaiah 14:13–15. How do these accounts help "flesh out" Proverbs 16:18?

5. Read Job 12:17, 20, 24–25 and Proverbs 21:30. In the end, does reliance on human wisdom "work?" Read 1 Corinthians 1:18–25. What do people consider "foolishness," but God considers "wisdom"?

The Day of the Lord

Verse 15 of Obadiah's little book mentions "the day of the LORD." This term is used in the Scriptures to refer to the day when Yahweh will intervene decisively for His people by delivering her from her enemies and bringing them to justice. Those who have not trusted in the Lord and His ultimate Deliverer (v. 21), will experience God's retributive justice: they will get what they deserve (see Exodus 21:23–25).

In Christ our Deliverer, we do not get what we deserve, but rather what He deserves: eternal blessing, honor, righteousness, and peace, through faith in His sacrifice. In turn, He received what we deserved on the cross, bearing our sins, suffering even hell itself. Although Obadiah does not mention Christ specifically, his words draw us to other passages of Scripture in which we see the Savior's work.

6. Compare verse 7c with Psalm 41:9. Who is speaking in John 13:18, 26–27? How is the "day of the LORD" described in Zechariah 14:1–9 and 1 Thessalonians 4:13–18? Whose coming do these passages announce?

7. Compare verse 21 to Revelation 11:15. What do they describe? Read Hebrews 12:22–29. Where can we go today to take part already in the blessings of Mount Zion? Knowing this, how might we be "servants of the LORD" like the prophet Obadiah?

In Closing

Encourage participants to begin the following activities:

- Read the book of Obadiah. Review the story of Esau (Edom), and his relationship to his younger brother Jacob (Israel), in Genesis 25:19–34; 27:1–46; 33:1–20; and 35:28–36:43.
- Read Jonah 1 to prepare for the next lesson.

Close with prayer.

Lesson 2

Jonah: Reluctant Missionary

God looks for people to serve Him as missionaries because He offers the Gospel of His grace and salvation to all people through His Word proclaimed by such persons. He has therefore commanded all Christians collectively to make disciples of all nations by baptizing and teaching. Individual Christians do this as they go about their daily tasks, come in contact with other people, and share the story of Jesus. But through the church, God calls persons into full-time service to proclaim Law and Gospel to those that are on the way to hell. Whatever work God has for the individual Christian to do, He wants only willing workers in His service. This is what the first chapter of Jonah teaches us.

Jonah's Call

Jonah begins abruptly with God's command for Jonah to leave his home country, where he had labored as a prophet, and go to Nineveh, the capital of the mighty Assyrian Empire. The purpose of his journey was to warn the people of that heathen city that God would punish them for the horrible sins they had committed. God's command terrified Jonah, for not only had God never asked this of any prophet before, but in Jonah's eyes this assignment was also most dangerous and unpleasant.

To get to Nineveh, Jonah would have to travel a long distance across wild and desert country. The city lay five hundred miles northeast of Jerusalem, on the east bank of the Tigris River. Nineveh was one of the oldest cities in the world, having been built by Asshur about 2,200 years before Christ, or 1,400 years before Jonah (Genesis 10:11). In Jonah's day it was also the largest city of the world, having a circumference of about 60 miles and a population of about 600,000 (3:3; 4:11). Ancient historians refer to the great size and the high, broad walls of Nineveh. Excavations have disclosed that it was indeed a very large city. The size of this capital city would not have mattered so much, had it not been for the kind of people that lived there and the fact that the Israelites feared and hated them. At that time Assyria was rapidly becoming a great world empire through ruthless conquest. The Assyrians had already conquered many nations and deported the captives. The people of Israel had good reasons to fear that someday they, too, would be carried off into captivity by the Assyrians (this actually happened in 722 B.C.). So nothing would have pleased Jonah more than if God had destroyed Nineveh—without any warning—as He had destroyed Sodom (Genesis 18:20; 19:24–25).

8. How was Jonah commissioned to be a foreign missionary? How was St. Paul commissioned (Acts 13:2–4)? How are missionaries called today? In what respect does the call of our missionaries to do mission work differ from the call every Christian has to share the Good News?

Avoiding the Mission Field

Jonah did not like the assignment God gave him. It was contrary to his feelings as an Israelite to warn the Ninevites of God's punishment and thus give them a chance to repent and be spared. That was evidently God's purpose (4:2). Jonah believed that the Gentiles were unworthy of God's grace and that God should let them perish in their sins and be destroyed. Rather than help the Ninevites by obeying God's command, Jonah decided to disobey God and go as far away from Nineveh as possible—in the opposite direction.

Jonah hurried to Joppa (modern Jaffa), a seaport on the Mediterranean 35 miles northwest of Jerusalem. Here he booked passage on a ship leaving for Tarshish (evidently Tartessus in Spain), about 2,500 miles to the west, beyond the Straits of Gibraltar. In ancient times the Atlantic Ocean was thought to be the western end of the world. Jonah was willing to pay a large sum of money for such a trip in order to get as far away as possible from his place of duty.

9. Why did Jonah not want to go to Nineveh (4:2)? Had Jonah ceased to be a true believer? Explain.

10. Twice we read in 1:3 that Jonah fled "from the presence of the LORD." Did he not know that God is everywhere (Psalm 139:7–10)? How can we explain that Jonah thought he could get away from the Lord? What fact is expressed in Psalm 139:7–10? When do we act like Jonah?

Stopped by a Storm

If Jonah thought God could not find him on the sea, he was badly mistaken. For a time he may have felt safe. Having nothing to do, he slept soundly in his cabin. But suddenly God caused a hurricane-like storm to strike the sea and churn its waves in mad fury. The ship's sailors had never experienced such a storm on the Mediterranean. Although they were unbelievers, they soon became convinced that a mighty god had sent this storm to punish someone guilty of a great sin. These hardened mariners became so terrified that everyone cried aloud to some pagan god for help. The captain even roused Jonah out of his sleep and urged him to pray to his God. How strange that an unbeliever here had to remind a prophet of the true God of his duty to pray! But we are not told that Jonah prayed.

Unbelievers thought that whenever there was a grave disaster, the gods were pursuing some great sinner who was trying to escape justice (Acts 28:4). Since all men are sinners and guilty before God, Christians should not blame others for the misfortunes they have to suffer (Luke 13:1–5). But here was a special case where God wanted to bring the sin of Jonah to light. He caused Jonah to be exposed by means of the lot (Proverbs 16:33).

It was a custom of unbelievers to seek from their gods what they wished to know by casting lots. On rare and exceptional occasions God's people in Bible times sought in this way to get an answer from the Lord. (There is only one instance in the New Testament when the lot was used: Acts 1:26.) Since we Christians have God's will revealed in His Word, we are not to seek to know more of it by employing other means. But the sailors were shocked and terrified when they heard how this prophet had dared to disobey his great and mighty God.

11. What experiences on this same Mediterranean did the apostle Paul have nine centuries after Jonah (Acts 27:14–44)? Contrast the apostle to Jonah. How did Jonah's sleep on the ship (1:5) differ from Christ's sleep on the Sea of Galilee (Matthew 8:24)?

12. How does our story prove that it is wrong for Christians to "hide their light under a bushel" (Matthew 5:14–16)? The unbelieving captain had to tell Jonah to pray; are our friends and family able to recognize us as praying Christians?

The Sign of Jonah

The frightened sailors were at a loss how they could appease Jonah's angry God. Therefore they turned to Jonah, expecting him to know what to do. Since the storm was raging on his account, he was certain that unless he sacrificed himself, the lives of all on board the ship would be lost. But the sailors did not want to take his advice and throw him overboard; it was against their conscience to kill a man in order to save themselves. Not until they saw that this was evidently God's will and they had prayed to Him to forgive them for committing such a horrible deed, did they carry out Jonah's instructions. As soon as Jonah had sunk into the waters, the sea became perfectly calm. This was overwhelming proof to the sailors that the Lord was Almighty God, and they worshiped Him and promised to serve Him.

But what had become of Jonah? God had further use for him; so He did not let him perish in the sea. The Lord caused a great fish to be at hand to swallow Jonah alive (1:17). For several days the repentant prophet found himself in most horrifying and unpleasant circumstances. But owing to the remarkable miracle wrought by the Lord, his life was preserved and he escaped drowning (and death), and finally reached land again.

13. What noble traits did the sailors reveal when they were told that they could save their own lives only by sacrificing Jonah (1:14)? In what respect is Jonah here a type of Christ (John 11:50–52)? How did Jonah unwittingly become a missionary to his heathen companions on the ship?

14. What would you tell someone claiming that this story cannot possibly be true? Explain why we accept this story as a great miracle. Why do we regard Jonah's confinement in the fish's body as a typical prophecy of Christ (Matthew 12:40; 16:4)? How do we understand the expression "three days and three nights," especially in the case of Christ? What comfort do Christians derive from the fact that Jonah's life was preserved in a miraculous manner (Psalm 139:9–11)?

In Closing

Encourage participants to begin the following activities:

- Begin reading about the ministry of Old Testament prophets. (For example, 1 Kings 17–2 Kings; 2 Chronicles 10–36; Ezra; Nehemiah; Isaiah–Malachi.)
- Read Jonah 2 to prepare for the next lesson.

Close with prayer.

Lesson 3

Prayer and Deliverance

One can hardly conceive of a more horrifying experience than Jonah's confinement for three days in the sea creature. Although his distress and discomfort were great, his faith had become fully revived, and as a child of God he prayed constantly to the Lord. Chapter 2 is a prayer of thanksgiving written down by the prophet as a poem after his deliverance. Remarkably, Jonah did not cry for help, but thanked God as though he were already delivered.

God Answers Prayer

Jonah 2:1 indicates how Jonah spent his time in the fish's stomach. The fact that he was now again able to pray shows that the runaway prophet had again turned to God and was eagerly clinging to Him as his personal God ("his" God).

Twice, in 2:2, Jonah states that he cried unto the Lord and that the Lord heard him. Here Jonah begins to cast his words in poetic form, using the Hebrew method of repeating the same thought by parallelism. The first half of this verse is almost a literal quotation from Psalm 120:1, while the other half reminds one of Psalm 18:6. Both quotations, however, were altered to fit the special situation of the prophet. With "from the depths of the grave" (Sheol), Jonah here means the realm of death (Psalm 30:3). Being in the fish seemed to Jonah to be as terrible as being in the realm of death.

15. How does the very beginning of chapter 2 indicate Jonah's change of heart? What does this teach about the value of affliction? Why should a Christian not confine his prayers to times and places that are pleasant and comfortable? Give examples.

Jonah's Horrible Experience

We may regard 2:3–5 as the first stanza of Jonah's hymn of prayer and thanksgiving. Here the prophet describes his terrifying experiences as he sank into the sea. Numerous parallel expressions in verse 3 (the deep; midst of the seas; floods; billows; waves) describe graphically the horrors that seized upon Jonah as he sank down to the bottom of the sea. In this description the words of Psalm 42:7 are utilized.

Jonah thought that God had now cast him out of His sight forever (v. 4). At that moment the words of Psalm 31:22 came to his mind, but since this passage also expresses the hope of deliverance, he found comfort in it and in the assurance given in Psalm 5:7. His renewed faith reached out to the little word *yet* ("nevertheless") and clung to that as a drowning man grasps a life preserver. Still feeling himself alive, he confidently believed that God would enable him once more to worship Him in the temple at Jerusalem.

But Jonah was sinking down deeper and deeper until he reached the very bottom of the sea (vv. 5–6). There seaweed entwined itself about him, threatening to hold him fast forever.

16. Perhaps you have known people who have narrowly escaped death. Why was such an experience unable to drive Jonah to despair (v. 4, see also Psalms 31:22; 5:7)? What advantage does a believer have over an unbeliever in the face of death? Why should a Christian not fear death?

Jonah's Comfort and Hope

The second stanza of the prayer (2:6–7) records Jonah's revival of hope as his thoughts turned to his God and he felt himself secure in His hands. There were indeed no prospects that he would ever emerge alive from that deep watery grave. But when all hope seemed to be gone, Jonah still had that blessed *yet* (v. 4) of God's Word to which his faith could cling. He saw his prayer answered and his faith vindicated when God suddenly caused him to be swallowed by the big fish and thus preserved his life. Now he could rejoice—even in the dark cavern of the creature—that the Lord was again his gracious God. He recalled the thoughts of grace and love which God has toward the sinner. His despondent heart was cheered by the Word of God that came to his mind. The fact that the Lord had preserved him from drowning was sufficient assurance to him that he would again be returned to dry land and would be able to worship the Lord in His temple. The sentiment he expressed in these verses was taken in part from Psalms 18:6, 69:1, 30:3, 40:2, 142:3, 143:4, and 88:3.

17. How did Jonah's faith in the Lord help him when he was at the bottom of the sea? What kept his faith alive and strong in such a hopeless situation? What lesson does this teach us? What does the Bible teach about the hope of Christians? (See Romans 5:3, 5; 8:24, 38, 39; 1 Corinthians 15:19–22; 1 Peter 1:3–5; Hebrews 11:1.)

Jonah Rededicates Himself

The third, and final, stanza (2:8–9) of Jonah's prayer rings out in a hymn of praise and thanksgiving, because he is fully assured of the Lord's goodness and mercy. God had set him aright; he was eager to proclaim loudly His praises and to dedicate himself entirely to His service. Luther points out that nothing is said of Jonah having made some special vow. He takes this promise to mean that Jonah promised to praise the Lord and preach His name for having delivered him (Psalms 116:17–19; 50:14, 15, 23).

Jonah concludes his prayer with the words "Salvation comes from the Lord" (v. 9). That is the sum of his experience and of his faith. God's thoughts toward man are thoughts of grace and salvation (Jeremiah 29:11).

18. Why is it an important part of the Christian life that we praise and thank God? How is this to be done? What kind of vows should we make to God? (See Matthew 4:10; Romans 14:8.) What vow did we make at our Baptism and renew at our confirmation? Discuss in what ways Christians can dedicate or consecrate themselves to God.

Jonah's Deliverance

At His appointed time the Lord caused Jonah to be cast forth unharmed out of the sea creature and to be returned to dry land (v. 10). This miracle may have taken place near Joppa. Jonah remembered the day when he had been cast into the sea and the day when he was delivered (1:17). Nature obeys God and renders Him willing service. But man must also be obedient to God and do His bidding; that was the lesson which Jonah now had learned. That is a lesson the Lord again and again needs to teach us too.

In Closing

Encourage participants to begin the following activities:

- Read how Jesus used the Psalms when He was on the cross. See Matthew 27:46 (Psalm 2:1) and Luke 23:46 (Psalm 31:5).
- Read Jonah 3 to prepare for the next lesson.

Close with prayer.

Lesson 4

Missionary Success

Jonah had learned one important lesson from his recent experiences: in the middle of his distress, God was still merciful. But he still had another lesson to learn, for he had not yet given up the idea that God should let the Gentiles perish in their sins. We would think that a person who had experienced God's mercy in such a miraculous way would be most eager to tell everyone else about his gracious God. Jonah was not that kind of missionary as yet. However, the Lord gave him the special training that he still needed.

Jonah's Second Call to Preach

By his flight Jonah had, so to speak, turned down the Lord's first call. However, God was still determined that Jonah should go to Nineveh; therefore He extended to him a second call (3:1). Jonah did the right thing by waiting until he knew what God wanted him to do. The Lord, with good reasons, might have decided to send someone else. Now Jonah knew that God wanted just him to be His messenger to Nineveh.

The first call had charged him to "preach against Nineveh," that is, to proclaim to the people that their sins had called the wrath of God down upon them (Jonah 1:2). This time (3:2), Jonah is merely told to "proclaim to it." It seems that the Lord purposely left His prophet in ignorance about what he should preach in Nineveh, so that he would be more willing to go and would abide by the divine instructions. He was to content himself with having a divine call; the message that he was to proclaim he would receive from God after his arrival in Nineveh.

19. Explain how God keeps calling us Christians like Jonah. Only Jonah's preaching could save Nineveh; how does this remind us of our

responsibility (Ezekiel 3:18)? Show that no one has a right to preach or teach anything but God's Word (Matthew 28:20).

Jonah Preaches in Nineveh

This time Jonah went (3:3). In God's eyes Nineveh was a great city (1:2; 4:11). Luther finds in this expression the idea that God had singled out Nineveh for a special manifestation of His mercy. "A day's journey" was the equivalent of about twenty miles; hence greater Nineveh had a circumference of sixty (some think ninety) miles. Modern excavations corroborate this statement regarding the size of Nineveh.

Jonah probably did not walk through the city in a straight line. He undoubtedly spent a whole day walking first along one street and then along another. Moving from one part of the city to another, he addressed the people wherever he could gather a crowd. He cried loudly so that all could hear. He certainly told them that the Lord had sent him; the Ninevites may also have heard of his miraculous escape from the sea. Jonah apparently preached only the Law; nevertheless, the Ninevites must have learned that the Lord is a merciful God. The fact that the exact time when Nineveh would be destroyed was revealed, and that this time was short, made Jonah's message the more terrifying and impressive (Genesis 6:3).

20. Do our missionaries perform their tasks "in obedience to the word of the Lord"? Explain. (See Acts 1:8; 13:2, 4.) What practice of evangelism did the apostles follow? (See Acts 18:4, 7; 19:8–9.) What was Jonah's message? What message do we have? (See Acts 2:38; 4:12; 16:31; John 3:16; Mark 16:16.)

The Entire City Repents

In 3:5–9 we have one of the most glorious reports of missionary success ever recorded. Whether or not Jonah's heart was in his work, in a short time the whole city became converted through his preaching. He could not have reached the ears of several hundred thousand people directly, but everyone who heard him passed on his words and thus became a missionary to others. The words that Jonah had spoken spread like wildfire all over the city and were even brought to the attention of the king in the palace. His message filled their hearts with terror, and they admitted that they deserved to be punished for their sins. Jonah says, in verse 5, that they "believed God" (the same wording used here in the original as in Genesis 15:6), and Jesus declared that the Ninevites had truly and sincerely repented (Luke 11:32).

To repent means to be sorry for one's sins (sincere remorse) and to turn to God for forgiveness (faith). Repentance involves a complete change of heart. An outward show of sorrow over sin is pleasing to God only when it is the expression of true sorrow in the heart; otherwise it is hypocrisy. But the Ninevites were sincere when they followed the ancient custom of fasting and wearing coarse clothing (sackcloth) as signs of humiliation, sorrow, and penitence. Even the king humbled himself, laid aside his royal apparel, sat in ashes, and in a special decree called upon all his subjects to observe a period of fasting, penitence, and prayer. Food and drink were to be kept from the animals, so that their cries, too, might ascend to heaven as prayers for mercy.

The main thing that the king stressed was that every individual should change his life, give up his sins, and turn to God (v. 8). It seems that the Ninevites had suddenly given up all their worship of idols (perhaps Jonah had rebuked their idolatry). It is evident that their whole change of conduct was the result of their having come to faith in the Lord. We are not to understand verse 9 as though they had doubts about God and His willingness to forgive them. They had no assurance that the Lord would spare their city even if they did repent; they could only hope that He would withhold from them the temporal punishment which they still deserved (an example of praying conditionally for earthly blessings).

21. How do we know that the Ninevites experienced a true conversion and turned to God in faith (v. 5; see also Luke 11:32)?

Explain the purpose of fasting, wearing sackcloth, and sitting in ashes. Does God expect that we show our repentance in this way when we are truly penitent? How should a Christian pray when he asks God to avert some great evil? (See Matthew 8:2; Luke 22:42; 2 Samuel 12:13–23.)

God Spares Nineveh

The Lord was pleased with the repentance of the Ninevites (3:10), and He decided not to destroy their city at this time. He "saw what they did," that is, their complete change of heart and life, which were the good fruits that resulted from their heeding His Word and believing in Him. He "had compassion" on them; this is not to be understood as though God changes His mind (see 1 Samuel 15:29). The Bible often speaks of God as it does people (Genesis 6:6). When God threatens to punish, He foresees how people will react to His threats, and He takes this into consideration. His holiness and justice demand that He punish sinners, but His love, grace, and mercy move Him to forgive them and withhold punishment when they turn to Him in repentance and faith (Lamentations 3:22, 33).

22. Some Christians use verse 10 to support their false teaching that people are saved by their good works. Why must we declare this claim to be contrary to Scripture (Hebrews 11:6)? What was the reason why God did not carry out His threat to destroy Nineveh?

23. What lesson does this passage teach us (a) with respect to ourselves; and (b) with respect to our sharing the Good News? Explain the purpose of Christ's warning in Luke 11:30, 32. See also Luke 12:48; Matthew 8:11–12.

In Closing

Encourage participants to begin the following activities:

- Read 1 Peter 2:4–10 and consider the job we have as spiritual priests to declare God's wonders.
- Read Jonah 4 to prepare for the next lesson.

Close with prayer.

Lesson 5

Prejudice and Rebuke

The story of Jonah now takes a surprising turn. We would expect Jonah to have been overjoyed at the conversion of Nineveh. Instead, we see that this glorious outcome only made the prophet disgruntled, bitter, and angry with God. What a strange missionary and prophet of God Jonah was! But the Lord still needed to drive home the lesson that He wanted to teach Jonah, the Israelites, and even us today. That is why the Book of Jonah was written and included in the Bible.

Jonah Offended at God's Mercy

In 4:10 Jonah is pictured as boiling over with anger ("was greatly displeased"). In a rather peculiar prayer he says that he has not found the Lord to be the kind of God he expected. In effect, Jonah might have said, "You have sent me here to prophesy that Nineveh would be destroyed in forty days; now you have made me to look like a false prophet, who cannot be trusted." However, Jonah's reputation was not the sole reason he was provoked. It was too much for him to see God show mercy toward people whom he disliked: the Gentiles. He angrily disapproved of the Lord being the gracious and merciful God He had proclaimed Himself to be (Exodus 34:6; see also Psalm 103:8–18). Jonah had forgotten that the Lord had dealt most mercifully with him. By fleeing from his call he had hoped that God would be unable to spare Nineveh. Now that the thing which he dreaded had come to pass, he sought to justify his disobedience.

While Jonah was quarreling with God, he peevishly prayed to be taken out of this world at once (v. 3). His angry outburst was a great sin, yet he prayed for a blessed end. Perhaps this implies that he no longer wished to serve God as a prophet on earth (as much as: "What is the use?"). What is most surprising in our text is God's boundless patience with Jonah (v. 4). He merely appeals to Jonah's conscience with the searching question: "Are you really justified in being angry at

Me?" This silences Jonah but does not move him to admit that he is wrong.

24. Why was Jonah's conduct senseless and sinful? Why should he have been thankful and happy that he knew God as He had revealed Himself in Exodus 34:6 and similar passages? How should this knowledge affect his attitude toward others? What causes us to act unfriendly and cold toward others? What is your opinion of Jonah's prayer (v. 3)? What was the purpose of God's question (v. 4)?

Jonah's Primary Concern

The Lord had undoubtedly revealed to Jonah that He would spare Nineveh. Since his work was done, Jonah had no reason for staying any longer at Nineveh. But he preferred remaining near that city until the period of forty days was up, hoping that what he had predicted might still come true. God did not interfere with Jonah's plans because they would serve Him to cure the prophet of his primary concern: himself.

Jonah selected a spot at a safe distance east of the city from which he could conveniently look down upon it (4:5). Here he erected a temporary hut of branches ("shelter") which gave him some protection from the hot sun. To add to his comfort and to show that He had not forgotten him, the Lord caused a shrub, or vine, to spring up overnight (v. 10) and to spread its leaves as an umbrella over Jonah's head. It is not certain what kind of plant this was. Some think it was the castor-oil plant (*ricinus*), which grows very rapidly and has broad leaves; others say it was the *palmcrist*, a plant that grows in India. Whatever the habits of the plant might be, it was only by a miracle of God that it reached its full growth in so short a time. Jonah was happy over this special gift of God, and this helped to calm his ugly mood.

But then suddenly Jonah was deprived of this precious comfort (v. 7). During the night God caused a worm to puncture the plant at its roots, and by morning it had withered and died. As a result Jonah became so irritable and grumpy that he wished for death. He became completely disgusted with life. When the Lord asked him whether he had just reason for taking the loss of the plant so much to heart, Jonah bitterly answered that he had good cause to be angry and to wish himself dead. What a poor, miserable sinner Jonah was!

25. What was God's purpose in causing the vine to grow over Jonah's head? What was miraculous about this? Why does the Lord provide us with certain comforts?

God Rebukes Jonah's Prejudice

The Lord had meant the incident of the vine to serve Jonah as an object lesson. Now He drove home that lesson with full force. Here was a plant that lived only for a few days, yet Jonah made so much fuss over its loss. In Nineveh there were 120,000 children under the age of seven (too young to distinguish between right and left). Since this age group normally comprises about one fifth of the population of a city, Nineveh must have sheltered about 600,000 people. The eternal loss of so great a number is of greatest concern to the compassionate Lord. He even takes into consideration the many animals since they are also His creatures and depend on Him for their life and being (Psalm 145:9, 15).

With this indisputable argument of the Lord the Book of Jonah closes. Jonah is speechless. "What could he have answered?" wrote Luther; he was "overcome by his own verdict." God always has the last word. His purpose was achieved. Jonah had now learned his lesson, as is evident from the story. Jonah committed it to writing under divine inspiration. He teaches us the lesson that God wants all men to be saved.

26. How did the Lord expose Jonah's prejudice as sinful? Explain how He taught Peter and the Jewish Christians the same lesson (see Acts 10:14, 15, 28, 34; 11:18). Why should Christians not be guilty of racism or look down upon any person (Galatians 3:28; Ezekiel 33:11; 1 Timothy 2:4; 2 Peter 3:9)? How did God reveal to Jonah His great love for all men, including the Gentiles? Why did Jonah remain silent after the Lord had spoken? God showed mercy even to the animals in

Nineveh. Explain why this should prompt us to be kind toward animals (Proverbs 12:10).

In Closing

Encourage the participants to begin the following activities:

- Read Nahum 3 and Zephaniah 2 to discover what later happened to Nineveh.
- Discuss the importance of daily repentance in the heart of a believer (1 John 1:8–9).
- Read Micah 1 to prepare for the next lesson.

Close with prayer.

Lesson 6

Micah: Preacher of Promise

Some people believe a Christian pastor should preach only the sweet Gospel and refrain from preaching the harsh Law. They believe that God should be pictured only as the God of love. But just as it would be a grave mistake for a farmer to cast seed upon an unplowed field, so, too, would the Christian pastor err by offering the Gospel to hardened impenitent hearts before applying the sharp till blade of the Law. The prophet Micah, whose name means "Who is like the LORD?" (see 7:18), did not make such a mistake, as little as did any of God's preachers in the Bible. We still need this kind of preaching today.

God's Punishment of Samaria and Jerusalem

In Micah's time the Northern Kingdom (Israel) and the Southern Kingdom (Judah) were morally rotten and spiritually dead. Represented by their capitals, Samaria and Jerusalem, they were so corrupt that the Lord could no longer allow them to go unpunished. All the kings of the Northern Kingdom had been ungodly men, and most of their subjects had followed them in serving idols and practicing shameful vices. At least some of the rulers of Judah were good kings, who served the Lord and encouraged their people to live godly lives. Thus Judah did not fall into spiritual decay as rapidly as its northern neighbor and continued much longer as an independent nation. But under Ahaz, the Southern Kingdom became so corrupt that it, too, was ripe for judgment. It was for this reason that the Assyrians led the northern tribes of Israel into captivity (722 B.C.), and the last remaining tribe of the Hebrews was led into captivity by the Babylonians (586 B.C.). All this Micah saw coming and foretold in our chapter as a warning to the Jews.

The prophet begins his pronouncement of the doom of the two countries with the loud cry: "Hear, O peoples, all of you" (1:2). What he says here about the punishment of the two Hebrew nations should serve as a warning example to all people (see Isaiah 1:2; Jeremiah 22:29). In verses 5–7 the prophet explains why the God's patience with these two countries has come to an end and why this terrible destruction in the Holy Land is to take place. The people boasted they were descendants of Jacob, the great patriarch. But they were far from living as his true children. They had become disloyal to the God of Jacob and were worshiping false gods at pagan altars. Therefore (v. 6) the glorious city of Samaria, built and adorned by Omri (1 Kings 16:24), would be turned into a heap of rubble, and where it stood vineyards would be planted. The carved images of idols, the many idol altars, and everything that pertained to idol worship, by the use of which Israel had proven itself unfaithful to the Lord, would be destroyed or carried off by the heathen invaders.

27. When God sends affliction upon one locality, He thereby warns all people on earth (see Deuteronomy 32:1; Isaiah 1:2; Jeremiah 22:29; Luke 13:1–5). What should people who continue to live securely in sin learn from our text? What does Micah preach to those claiming to be Christians but whose hearts are attached to money, entertainment, and other earthly things, as their idols? How does God prove in wars and conflicts that He still punishes nations which are ripe for judgment?

The Sad State of Israel

Verses 8–16 are peculiar and somewhat difficult to understand because Micah uses picture language and refers to things unfamiliar to us. First, he shows how deeply the punishment which his people are to suffer affects him. He then calls up all his countrymen to mourn and lament with him in the spirit of true repentance. Micah feels that this lamentation should be very pronounced, like the doleful cries of a jackal in the desert and the plaintive calls of the ostrich. Like Isaiah, he speaks of his nation as wounded unto death, utterly helpless and ruined because of its sins (Isaiah 1:5–7). He sees the enemy that has destroyed Samaria marching upon Jerusalem to lay it to waste in verse 9.

In verses 10–15 Micah rebukes the ungodly of his nation by means of a whole string of puns (in the original Hebrew). He plays upon the names of certain places in a way that expresses bitter irony, because the people would not listen to God until it was too late: *Gath* means "announcement" (v. 10); *Beth Ophrah* means "house of dust" (v. 10); *Saphia* means "pleasant" (v. 11); *Zaanan* means "outlet" (v. 11); *Beth Ezel* means "house of separation" (v. 11); *Maroth* sounds like *bitter* (v. 12); *Lachish* means "team" (v. 13); *Moresheth Gath* means "the betrothed of Gath" (v. 14); *Achzib* means "deception" (v. 14); *Mareshah* sounds like *conqueror* (v. 15).

Verse 16 is an appeal of the prophet to his people to mourn and repent over their sins. A special sign of grief and mourning in the Middle East was to shear or shave one's head. The nation made bald by devastation is told to mourn in this fashion over the fact that its young children were being led away into captivity. Here Micah is thinking not only of the Assyrian invasion under Sennacherib, but of the Babylonian Captivity.

28. Discuss the figurative expressions and the puns which Micah employs in this second section. Why would Micah express himself in this poetic manner? It is apparent that much of this was meant to be bitter irony. Why would the prophet feel that way toward his people?

In Closing

Encourage participants to begin the following activities:

- Read and discuss the comforting truths Micah offers in 4:3–5; 5:2–4; 7:7; 18–20.
- Compare Micah 1:15 with 1 Samuel 22 to learn more about Adullom.
- Read Micah 2 to prepare for the next lesson.

Close with prayer.

Lesson 7

The Coming King

Every person's religion is reflected in the life that he or she leads. A Christian will show by his or her conduct that he or she is a godly, upright, and virtuous human being. His or her entire life is devoted to serving God and promoting the welfare of others. But the very opposite is the case with all who do not believe. Such people can only bring forth the fruits of ungodliness that fill their sinful hearts. That is the kind of people Micah had to deal with in his day. Although they claimed to be the chosen people of God, they had turned their backs upon Him and His Word. Therefore it is not surprising that they lived very sinful and offensive lives.

The Sins of Greed and Injustice

Having announced God's judgment upon the two Hebrew nations because of their idolatry (1:3–16), Micah now addresses the wealthy, the upper classes, and leaders of his country (2:1–5). He describes them as cunning schemers who spent their nights planning how they could fleece others during the day. Their covetousness knew no bounds. By means of force and injustice they seized upon the property of the poor, the possessions God had given to His people for their inheritance (Exodus 20:17).

This greed of the Israelites not only aroused the indignation of the prophet, but also caused him to warn them of God's punishment. The Lord would not tolerate this evil, but would punish these robbers with a great evil that He would send upon them. All their wealth will be stripped from them and they will be taken as prisoners to Assyria or Babylon. In their captivity they will have to listen to the mockery of their captors who will give them plenty of cause to wail and lament over the loss of their homeland. Not even a measuring line (cord) will be of any use to them, since they will not be able to buy and possess land of their own in captivity (v. 5).

29. Would Micah have reasons for preaching against greed and oppression in our day? Explain. What stand does the Bible take toward covetousness? (See Exodus 20:17; Luke 12:15; Ephesians 5:5; 1 Timothy 6:9–10.)

False Prophets Increase Wickedness

The Israelites disliked Micah's preaching very much; they neither wanted to be rebuked by him for their sins nor to be told that God would give them into the hands of their enemies. In their opposition to Micah the influential people were supported by the false prophets, who flattered them and encouraged them to ridicule God's true prophet. Evidently these false prophets had said that Micah's threats could not be reconciled with the Lord's goodness and the special favor in which He held His chosen people. Micah meets that objection with the remark that God indeed has great patience but is nevertheless obliged to punish when people show no sign of repentance.

The reason why God threatens by His prophet is to be found in the wickedness of the people. Israel was living in open rebellion against the Lord. By their conduct the people were showing how little they cared about God. Without the least consideration for justice and the rights of others, they had stripped the clothing off peaceable people whom they met on the road, although they had no quarrel with them. They also deprived widows and orphans of their property and the blessings God had given them by claiming these for themselves as payment of the debts the widows had been obliged to make upon the death of their husbands. (See Exodus 22:25; Matthew 23:14.)

Micah declares that such criminal conduct as this must be punished by banishment from the land (2:10). Such stinging remarks like this by Micah would, of course, be very unwelcome to the wicked leaders. They much rather listened to the false prophets, who flattered them with their lies (v. 11). These men preached their own ideas and favored getting as much enjoyment out of this life as possible. For that reason they enjoyed public favor as popular preachers (2 Timothy 4:3–4).

30. Have people changed since Micah's time in their attitude toward the ministers of the Word? What kind of persons are the most popular preachers today? Why? What attitude do some take when they do not like what their pastor preaches? What kinds of promises do false teachers make? Why should we be discerning when listening, watching, or reading "Christian" radio, television, or books?

Believers Safe in the Good Shepherd's Care

In this, his first sermon, Micah has finished preaching the Law to the ungodly. He now concludes with a word of sweet comfort for the believers, to whom the prophets refer as "the remnant of Israel." God has at all times some who remain loyal to Him; this was true also in the days of Micah. When God punishes the wicked, He may permit the godly to suffer along with them. Many believing Jews had to wander into captivity (e.g., Daniel and his friends, Ezekiel). But God did not forsake them. He gave them cheering words of promise through His prophets.

We have the first of Micah's Messianic prophecies in 2:12–13. Here he addresses as "Jacob" the spiritual Israel, the true believers of all ages to come. The One speaking to them through Micah is the Messiah, who is a true man but at the same time God Himself. He will, in time, gather all believers as His sheep into the fold of His church. They will be well cared for by their Shepherd, as were the sheep in the rich grazing country of Bozra, east of the Jordan River. Into His fold Christ will bring not only Jews, but people from all nations (Gentiles). The church will finally grow into a mighty host, cause a great stir among men, and bring about great changes in the world.

31. Show that Micah is speaking only to the believers in this passage. Explain why this text is to be regarded as a messianic prophecy. Point out the similarity between this passage and John 10:14–16, 28, 30. Why are such references to Christ as "the Good Shepherd" most comforting?

In Closing

Encourage participants to begin the following activities:

- Discuss how Micah 2:12–13 proves that Christ is true God.
- Read Micah 3 to prepare for the next lesson.

Close with prayer.

Lesson 8

False Prophets Rejected

Micah's second sermon begins with chapter 3 and continues through chapters 4 and 5. Here, again, the prophet first preaches the Law and threatens the ungodly Israelites with divine punishment because of their sins. But in the two following chapters, Micah comforts the believers with more Gospel promises and assures them of salvation and eternal blessings in the kingdom of Christ.

Civil Rulers Brought to Justice

Here Micah takes the officials of his government severely to task (3:1–3). He implores them to hear what he has to say to them in particular. The "leaders of Jacob" were the elders, or rulers, of the various family groups, or households, whose duty it was to administer justice in their local communities. But they had been doing the very opposite of what was required of them. They had abused the authority of their official station by oppressing the poor and abandoning the way of justice. Their rule was contrary to what good government should be (Romans 13:3–4).

Micah 3:4 shows how terrible their punishment will be. When they go into captivity, they will suffer the same misery they had brought upon others, but the Lord will have no pity on them. Because they will not repent, but cry only for relief from their sufferings, God will not hear them nor have mercy on them (Proverbs 1:24–32).

32. What responsibility do all civil governments have with respect to their subjects? (See Romans 13:3–4; Deuteronomy 1:16–17.) What does the Bible say about wicked men in public office? (See

Proverbs 17:25; 24:23–24; 28:15; 29:2.) What warning does God give all wicked rulers in Proverbs 1:24–32?

Micah versus the False Prophets

Micah turns upon the prophets who deceived the people with their lies and shows what miserable spiritual leaders they were and what their fate will be (3:5–7). Although God had not sent them, they presumed to speak in the name of the Lord. They misled the people by preaching what pleased them instead of denouncing their sins (Jeremiah 6:14). As long as they were well fed (had something to bite with their teeth) and were bribed with money, they promised peace and good times. But they had it in for those who refused to contribute to their support. These they tried to terrify with predictions of evil and piously claimed that God would punish them. However, God's judgment would also overtake them and expose them as false prophets.

With respect to Micah and all true prophets of God, it is an altogether different story (v. 8). Micah could point to himself as a true spokesman of God, since he was filled with and inspired by the Holy Spirit (2 Peter 1:21). The Word he preached was not only true but also powerful. (See Romans 1:16; 2 Timothy 1:7.) He proclaimed the Lord's judgment, or divine right. In this divine strength he could pass judgment upon the sins of all the people and clearly predict God's punishment (Isaiah 58:1). Micah did not flatter the sinners, as the false prophets did, but preached the Law without fear or favor.

33. What is often the real reason why false prophets preach the things people like to hear (3:5)? How does Jesus describe them in Matthew 7:15? Explain the difference between a false prophet and a true minister of the Word with respect to their office, message, and reward. To what extent does verse 8 apply to all true pastors?

The Destruction of Jerusalem

As a true prophet Micah proclaims what God has given him to speak. With another "Hear this" he returns to the beginning of his sermon (3:9), but now to announce to the wicked leaders the punishment God has in store for them. They are condemned for their insatiable greed. The civil rulers have judged according to the bribes they received. The priests, who were to teach the law without pay, demanded fees for their teaching. (See Leviticus 10:11; Deuteronomy 17:11; Jeremiah 6:3.)

But Micah proclaims for them a day of reckoning (v. 12). Because of their sins Jerusalem would be laid in ruins; the palace grounds on Mount Zion would become tillable soil, the rest of the city piles of broken stones, the height on which the temple stood like the hills of a forest covered with brush. (See Isaiah 32:13–14; Lamentations 1.)

34. Some persons have built up great fortunes by exploiting the people and then have established fine buildings and institutions for the benefit of the public; what does Micah tell such people in our text? What must be said of persons who will work and serve others only if they are paid well or are offered a bribe? How does verse 12 prove that Micah was a true prophet of God?

In Closing

Encourage participants to begin the following activities:

- Compare Micah 3:12 to Jeremiah 26:16–19.
- Read Micah 4 to prepare for the next lesson.

Close with prayer.

Lesson 9

The Lord's Mountain

Although Micah condemned the ungodliness of the Israelites and told that they would be led into captivity, he was not a prophet of hopelessness and despair. He believed God's promises concerning salvation, which the Messiah would bring them. In spirit Micah looked far beyond the time of Israel's captivity in Babylon and the return of the Jews to Palestine—he saw what a blessed and happy people the believers during the long era of the New Testament church would be. He now describes the future glory of that church in almost the same language as used by the prophet Isaiah in his second chapter.

Christ's Kingdom

Micah had just pictured the destruction of Jerusalem as being so complete that it would resemble a plowed field and a forest (3:12). Now, in the fourth chapter, he seems suddenly to make of that city such a wonderful place that people from all over the world want to flock to it and find in it perfect and unending peace. However, the thoughtful reader of this chapter should be able to see that Micah's words here (similar to Isaiah 2:2–4) are not to be taken literally; they refer to the spiritual kingdom of Christ in the New Testament. That is why Micah says that all this will take place "in the last days," by which he means the whole period of the Christian church from the time of Jesus to the end of the world.

Micah first points to the prominent position which the Christian church will occupy in the world (4:1–2). All nations of the earth will eventually take note of it and come under its influence. (See Isaiah 40:9; Matthew 5:14–16.) The church is the spiritual Jerusalem, Zion, and temple, in which they hear the Law and the Gospel of God preached. Drawn by the Gospel, they flock, in ever-increasing numbers, into the church to become its members. (See Isaiah 60:1–6; John 4:35; Romans 11:25.) Hence, both Micah and Isaiah describe, in this figurative language, the conversion of the Gentiles throughout the New Testament era.

A literal interpretation of 4:3–7 has led people to make claims that contradict the plain teachings of the Bible. Many (millennialists, chiliasts) still cling to the idea that a time will come on earth when all people will be converted to Christ and that thereafter will follow a thousand years of perfect peace when no nation will think of waging war against another. But such dreams get no support from our passage nor from any other statement in Scripture. Micah is speaking only of the believers and describes the inward spiritual peace, harmony, and happiness, which they enjoy as "brothers and sisters" of whom the Gospel has made one family.

35. How may we explain Micah 4:1–2 in the light of Matthew 13:31–32? Note the similarity between Micah 4:1–2 and Isaiah 2:2–3. Would it make sense and be in harmony with Scripture if we adopted a literal interpretation of this passage? Explain. (See Luke 17:21; John 4:21–24; 10:16; Matthew 24:14; Hebrews 12:22–23.) Explain what Micah has in mind.

36. Can we expect, in the light of Scripture and experience, that a time will ever come on this earth when universal peace will prevail and when there will be no more wars? What success will all human efforts in this direction have according to Matthew 24:7–21; James 4:1; Romans 3:10–18; Matthew 15:19?

The Church Assured of Deliverance and Victory

In the second part of chapter 4 Micah sees that the church, which is all peace and glory within, will have to suffer much tribulation from without, but that Christ will eventually make it victorious over all its enemies (4:6–13). The church is the spiritual Zion in which Christ, the great descendant of David's royal line, has established His throne of grace and exercises His rule for its protection and welfare. As a mighty, protecting Fortress Christ shields His church, and as an alert Shepherd, He watches that no harm befalls any member of His flock.

The enemies of the church hope in vain for its destruction. Again and again they launch their attacks against it, and they rejoice when they see it suffering shame and degradation (v. 11). (See also 7:10; Psalm 137; Obadiah 11–13.) But they do not reckon with the fact that the Lord is chastening His people for a good purpose (v. 12). When He has purified His own in the fires of affliction, He will execute judgment upon the enemies of the church. Many who persecuted it will become humble and consecrated disciples of Christ and will glorify God, who is here called "the Lord of all the earth" (v. 13). (See also Philippians 2:11.)

37. How are the security and glory of the believers described in Micah 4:8? What important lessons does Micah 4 have for the church today?

In Closing

Encourage the participants to begin the following activities:

- In what ways does the church bear a cross (Acts 14:22)?
- Read Micah 5 to prepare for the next lesson.

Close with prayer.

Lesson 10

The Saving Shepherd

Micah has already spoken about the coming of the Messiah. Now, in chapter five, he gives the Old Testament church a more detailed picture of the Savior. This is what he says about Him: He will be born in Bethlehem; He will be both true God and true man; He will be the Ruler of the church and provide for it as a shepherd cares for his flock; He will extend His kingdom over the whole earth and will subdue all His enemies; He will be our peace. From the New Testament we know how exact and true the prophet's description of Christ is. It marks the highest point in Micah's book.

Micah's Christmas Message

The first verse of chapter 5 gives the proper setting for a beautiful message. The Savior was to appear at the time when Israel had reached the stage of its deepest misery and degradation (Genesis 49:10). What was once the chosen nation of God would then be helpless in the power of its enemies; it would be insulted and deprived of all its former glory. It would no longer have a king and government of its own.

But at the time of Israel's deepest humiliation, the greatest event in the history of mankind would take place: In Bethlehem would be born Christ, the Lord. Micah is so specific in giving important details that he mentions the very place of the Savior's birth. (See Matthew 2:6; John 7:42.) He would not be born in Jerusalem, the capital; for a stranger (Herod) would there be ruling instead of a descendant of David. As the Lord had once honored the little town of Bethlehem when He chose David to be king over Israel, so He would again honor it by making it the birthplace of His Son (1 Corinthians 1:26–29). Bethlehem ("House of Bread"), with the added name Ephrathah ("Fruitful"), seemed insignificant in the eyes of the world with its small population of less than a thousand families, yet it would give to the world the greatest person ever to walk on this earth (John 6:48).

38. Explain the meaning and purpose of 5:1. Show how degraded and miserable Israel was at the time Christ was born. (See Genesis 49:10; Isaiah 11:1; 53:2; Matthew 2:3.)

39. Share what you know about Bethlehem. (Refer to Genesis 35:19; Ruth 1:19; 4:11; 1 Samuel 17:12; Matthew 2:6; John 7:42.) How does Micah's statement about Bethlehem's small size (v. 2) compare with the significance given to it? Why did God select Bethlehem for the birthplace of His Son?

40. Show from verse 2 that the Messiah was to carry out God's plan of salvation. How does Micah indicate that He would be true God? Verse 3 mentions Christ's human mother. What else do we learn about her role from Isaiah 7:14, Matthew 1:18–23, and Galatians 4:4?

Good Shepherd and Prince of Peace

In 5:4–8 Micah shows what the Messiah will do for His people. He sees Christ standing firm and erect as one who possesses divine power and majesty and shows that He is the Lord Himself. Again Micah sees Him as a shepherd watching over and feeding His flock. (See Isaiah 40:11; 49:10; Ezekiel 34:23.) Micah sees the God-man wielding the power of God (also according to His human nature) on His throne in heaven. "Now," during the time of His exaltation, He extends His rule and kingdom over all parts of the earth.

This one person, Christ, and He alone, is the fountainhead of peace between God and man. (See Isaiah 9:6; Ephesians 2:14, 17; Colossians 1:15–23.) "The peace" is the state of intimate and blissful relationship between God and the believers, which Christ established.

He sends His "undershepherds," His servants who are anointed with the Holy Spirit, into the enemy countries to conquer them with the Gospel. In fact, Christ scatters the believers ("the remnant of Jacob") among the ungodly for a good purpose (vv. 7–8). In the end His church will triumph over all its enemies, either by winning them for Him or by striking terror into their hearts with God's judgments.

41. Show how Christ is described in 5:4 as the Great Ruler. Why does Micah frequently present the Messiah in the role of a shepherd? How can the Messiah be God and yet refer to the Lord as His God? (See John 20:17; 1:18.) How does Christ exercise His rule as the Prince of Peace (vv. 5–8)? What is the only way the church can win victory over its enemies? (See Romans 10:17; Isaiah 60:4–5.)

Christ Will Purify His Church

The church's foes are God's enemies; He will therefore help it to become victorious over them. But the church must remove all traces of worldliness from its own midst. When the Lord brings His church into great tribulation (vv. 10–14), He does this for the purpose of weaning the hearts of the Christians away from the vanities of this world and turning them to Him (Isaiah 9:4–6). The history of Israel serves as an illustration to show how necessary this is. Instead of relying solely upon God when the heathen hordes invaded their land, the Jews put their confidence in their military equipment and fortifications. To teach them how vain it is to trust in earthly things, the Lord caused their whole military might to collapse. He also purified the Old Testament church from all idolatrous practices by causing the false gods and their priests to be destroyed.

42. Explain why worldliness is the greatest danger to the church. How must it safeguard itself against this danger? Why is it important that Christians keep themselves unspotted from the world? (See James 1:27; 1 John 2:15–17; 2 Peter 3:14.)

In Closing

Encourage the participants to begin the following:

- Discuss Micah 5:15 in relation to Isaiah 66:24; Revelation 21:26–27; 22:15 in relation to the Last Day.
- Read Micah 6 to prepare for the next lesson.

Close with prayer.

Lesson 11

Justice and Mercy

In chapter six we come to Micah's third, and last, address. Once more he calls upon his people: "Listen" (v. 1). This time the Lord is speaking through His prophet words of fervent pleading and severe rebuke. It is as though God had filed a lawsuit against Israel and He is now calling upon them to state why they had become disloyal and ungrateful to Him. They cannot appease Him and regain His favor by means of offerings and sacrifices. No, they will be acceptable to Him only if they acknowledge Him as their highest Good and show by their conduct toward Him and their fellow men that they are His obedient and loving children (6:1–8).

In the second part of this chapter (6:9–16), the prophet again rebukes the Israelites for their selfishness, greed, and lack of love toward the underprivileged classes, and he threatens that God will punish them with captivity, famine, and public disgrace.

God's Case against Israel

In this passage we have the remarkable picture of the Lord arguing with His people, Israel, as we would talk to a friend who has repaid kindness with ingratitude and insults. Through Micah, He reminds His people of four great events in the history of Israel: the miraculous deliverance out of slavery in Egypt (Exodus 14); the gift of outstanding leaders such as Moses, Aaron, and Miriam; Balak and Balaam (Numbers 22–24); and the events at Shittim and Gilgal (Joshua 3:1; 4:9). Were these not great and wonderful manifestations of God's love for His people?

Micah also acts as the spokesman of the people and frames the answer they might give to God (6:6–7). Although they made no frank confession of their sins or show signs of repentance, they would be willing to increase their sacrifices, even burning their own children on the altars. But God told them that the right relationship between Him and man is not established by means of offerings and sacrifices (6:8). God demands of man the consecration of the heart to Him, a spiritual worship and service. According to the First Table the people should walk humbly and sincerely in true fellowship with God and gladly do His will (Ecclesiastes 12:13). And according to the Second Table they should do what is right toward their fellow men and serve them with deeds of love and charity.

43. What does this touching appeal of God to Israel (vv. 1–5) reveal to us about His attitude toward sinners? What answer could we give to verse 3?

44. Discuss 6:6–7 and how these sentiments of the Israelites reveal their self-righteousness and lack of a true spirit of worship. (See John 4:24; Psalm 50:7–14; Isaiah 1:11–17; Hosea 6:6.) Does God approve of human sacrifices? (See Deuteronomy 12:31; 2 Kings 3:27; Jeremiah 19:5; 32:35.) Of what significance to us is Micah 6:8?

Warning for the Wicked

In 6:9–16 God gives His people another earnest warning. Because Israel was living contrary to His demands in verse 8, He must come against them as their Judge and threaten them with punishment. Israel and Judah were ripe for judgment (vv. 10–16). The people were greedy. They were a nation of thieves, cheaters, and liars. Their shrewd and shady business practices were an abomination to the Lord.

Now follows what God threatens to do to those who practice dishonesty (vv. 13–16). He will inflict a terrible punishment upon them "because of their sins." He will give them a taste of their own medicine and make them suffer what they have done to others. (See Matthew 7:2; Galatians 6:7.) Also, in Judah, the people deserved such a terrible punishment because they had lived after the manner of the ungodly kings of Israel, Omri (1 Kings 16:16–28) and Ahab (1 Kings 21:25–26), who had introduced the shameful Baal worship into Israel. For this reason God would make the Israelites objects of horror, whom the heathen would jeer.

45. Describe the nature and value of true wisdom (v. 9). (See also Proverbs 9:10; 2:6; 4:4.) What does God teach people when He applies the rod of affliction?

46. Would the prophet have reasons for raising the same charge against our nation today as he did against the Jews (vv. 10–12)? How does God regard all dishonesty in business? (See Leviticus 19:35; Deuteronomy 25:13–16; Proverbs 11:1; 16:11.) Show why ill-gotten wealth brings no happiness (1 Timothy 6:9–10).

In Closing

Encourage participants to begin the following activities:

- Discuss Micah 6:8 and the "good" that God gives us.
- Read Micah 7 to prepare for the next lesson.

Close with prayer.

Lesson 12

Pardon and Forgiveness

In all three of his addresses Micah had fearlessly denounced the national sins of Israel and had announced the punishment that would overtake the ungodly and impenitent sinners. He knew that most of these would not listen to his warnings. So, in closing, he turns to the small "remnant" of believers and prepares them for the evil days through which they must pass. He ends his message and book with a mighty hymn of praise, declaring not only that there is but one God, the Lord, but also showing that His chief greatness consists in forgiving the sins of and keeping His promises to his often wayward people.

Repentance and Faith

In chapter 7 Micah speaks not for himself, but for the church. The believers of that time were saddened by the fact that their own number was so small and that everywhere they saw nothing but corruption and wickedness (vv. 1–6). This had made the nation ripe for the judgment, which the true prophets had prophesied. Human beings had become so depraved that they had no regard for the most sacred ties of human relationship. No one could trust his intimate friend or even his own wife. Children despised their parents, and the various members of a family were each other's enemies.

Over against this dark picture of the times, Micah testifies that he and the church do not put their confidence in men, but look unto the Lord and hope in His salvation, knowing that He will answer their prayer for grace and deliverance (v. 7). He will not forsake them; after He has disciplined them, He will again remove their distress, shine upon them in His grace, and prove to them that He remains faithful to His promises (Psalm 103:17). Looking again into the Messianic era, the prophet sees the church no longer confined to the land of Israel (vv.

11–17), but sees it winning converts from all nations, from Assyria and the Euphrates River to Egypt, from nations also beyond the seas.

47. Would we be justified in complaining today as Micah did in 7:2–6? Explain. What was Christ's purpose in quoting from Micah 7:6 in Matthew 10:35–36 (Luke 12:53)? What glorious hope do the believers have (v. 7)?

The Lord is a Great God

Micah begins the last part of his address with a fervent prayer to God, asking Him to be the Good Shepherd of His flock (7:8–14). He sees Christ, equipped with a shepherd's staff, going before His people and leading them to the green pastures of His Word. (See Psalm 23:4; Isaiah 40:11; Ezekiel 34:11–23; John 10:12–17.) Under Him the believers will have plenty of rich spiritual nourishment; they will be as well taken care of as were the sheep and cattle on the fertile hillsides of Mount Carmel and the pasturelands of Bashan and Gilead, east of the Jordan River (Jeremiah 50:19).

Micah has poured out his prayer before God. Now comes the Lord's answer (vv. 15–17). He promises more than the church has asked. During its New Testament period it will see God performing miracles even greater than the deliverance of Israel out of Egypt. Overwhelmed by this wonderful outlook, Micah now bursts forth with a sublime hymn of praise in honor of the great Lord God (vv. 18–20). He sees God's greatness in the fact that He forgives sins and delights to show mercy to those who have deserved nothing but eternal punishment. (See Exodus 34:6–7; Jonah 4:2; Psalm 103:8.)

48. Explain why no false god has ever been described as the Lord is described in verse 18. Show how the difference between the true religion (Christianity) and all false religions is stressed here. Why must we look to Christ if we wish to know what God is to us? (See John 3:16; 1:18; 14:9; 2 Corinthians 5:19.)

In Closing

Encourage the participants to begin the following activities:

- Compare Micah 7:14 to Psalm 23:4.
- Relate how Micah 7:18–20 and Isaiah 44:22 refer to Christ.

Close with prayer.

Leader Guide

This guide is provided as a "safety net," a place to turn for help in answering questions and for enriching discussion. It will not answer every question raised in your class. Please read it, along with the questions, before class. Consult it in class only after exploring the Bible references and discussing what they teach. Please note the different abilities of your class members. Some will easily find the Bible passages listed in this study; others will struggle. To make participation easier, team up members of the class. For example, if a question asks you to look up several passages, assign one passage to one group, the second to another, and so on. Divide the work! Let participants present the answers they discover.

Preparing to Teach Obadiah, Jonah, and Micah

To prepare to lead this study, read through the Books of Obadiah, Jonah, and Micah. You might secure good commentaries on the books and read them over or read the introduction to the books in *The Concordia Self-Study Bible* or a Bible handbook. Several maps showing the Old Testament world around 850–550 B.C. would also be of help.

The materials in these notes are designed to help you in leading others through this portion of the Holy Scriptures. Nevertheless, this booklet is to be an aid to and not a substitute for your own study of and preparation for teaching the Books of Obadiah, Jonah, and Micah.

If you have the opportunity, you will find it helpful to make use of other biblical reference works in the course of your study. These three commentaries can be very helpful: Paul R. Raabe, *Obadiah: A New Translation with Introduction and Commentary*, Anchor Bible Commentaries (New York: Doubleday, 1996); Leslie C. Allen, *The Books of Joel, Obadiah, Jonah, and Micah*, The New International Commentary on the Old Testament (Grand Rapids: Eerdmans, 1976); and Cyril W. Spaude, *Obadiah, Jonah, Micah*, The People's Bible Series (Milwaukee: Northwestern Publishing House, 1987; reprinted by Concordia Publishing House, 1994). Although it is not strictly a commentary, the sections on Obadiah, Jonah, and Micah in *The Word Becoming Flesh* by Horace Hummel (St. Louis: Concordia Publishing

House, 1979) also contain much that is of value for the proper interpretation of these biblical books.

Group Bible Study

Group Bible study means mutual learning from one another under the guidance of a leader. The Bible is an inexhaustible resource. No one person can discover all it has to offer. In any class many eyes see many things, things that can be applied to many life situations. The leader should resist the temptation to "give the answers" and so act as an "authority." This teaching approach stifles participation by individual members and can actually hamper learning. As a general rule don't "give interpretation," instead "develop interpreters." In other words, don't explain what the learners can discover by themselves. This is not to say that the leader shouldn't share insights and information gained by his or her class members during the lesson, or engage them in meaningful sharing and discussion or lead them to a summary of the lesson at the close.

Have a chalkboard and chalk or newsprint and marker available to emphasize significant points of the lesson. Rephrase your inquiries or the inquiries of participants as questions, problems, or issues. This provokes thought. Keep discussion to the point. List on the chalkboard or newsprint the answers given. Then determine the most vital points made in the discussion. Ask additional questions to fill gaps.

The aim of every Bible study is to help people grow spiritually, not merely in biblical and theological knowledge, but in Christian thinking and living. This means growth in Christian attitudes, insights, and skills for Christian living. The focus of this course must be the church and the world of our day. The guiding question will be this: What does the Lord teach us for life today through Obadiah, Jonah, and Micah?

Teaching the Old Testament

Teaching the Old Testament can degenerate into mere moralizing in which "do-goodism" becomes a substitute for the Gospel and sanctification gets confused with justification. Actually the justified sinner is not moved by God's Law but by God's grace to a totally new life. His or her faith in Christ is always at work in every context of life. Meaningful personal Christianity consists of faith flowing from God's grace in Christ and is evidenced in love for other people. Having experienced God's free grace and forgiveness, the Christian daily works in his or her world to reflect the will of God for humanity in every area of human endeavor.

The Christian leader is Gospel-oriented, not Law-oriented. He or she distinguishes Law from Gospel. Both are needed. There is no clear Gospel unless we first have been crushed by the Law and see our sinfulness. There is no genuine Christianity where faith is not followed by a life pleasing to God. In fact, genuine faith is inseparable from life. The Gospel alone creates in us the new heart that causes us to love God and our neighbor.

When Christians teach the Old Testament, they do not teach it as a "law-book," but instead as books containing both Law and Gospel. They see the God of the Old Testament as a God of grace who out of love establishes a covenant of mercy with His people (Deuteronomy 7:6–9) and forgives their sins. Christians interpret the Old Testament using the New Testament message of fulfilled prophecy through Jesus Christ. They teach as leaders who personally know the Lord Jesus as Savior, the victorious Christ who gives all believers a new life (2 Corinthians 5:17) and a new mission (John 20:21).

Pace Your Teaching

The lessons in this course of study are designed for a study session of at least an hour in length. If it is the desire and intent of the class to complete an entire lesson each session, it will be necessary for you to summarize the content of certain answers or biblical references in order to preserve time. Asking various class members to look up different Bible passages and to read them aloud to the rest of the class will save time over having every class member look up each reference.

Also, you may not want to cover every question in each lesson. This may lead to undue haste and frustration. Be selective. Pace your teaching. Spend no more than 5–10 minutes opening the lesson. During the lesson, get the sweep of meaning. Occasionally stop to help the class gain understanding of a word or concept. Allow approximately 5 minutes for "Closing" and announcements.

Should your group have more than a one-hour class period, you can take it more leisurely. But do not allow any lesson to drag and become tiresome. Keep it moving. Keep it alive. Keep it meaningful. Eliminate some questions and restrict yourself to those questions most meaningful to the members of the class. If most members study the text at home, they can report their findings, and the time gained can be applied to relating the lesson to life.

Good Preparation

Good preparation by the leader usually affects the pleasure and satisfaction the class will experience.

Suggestions to the Leader for Using the Study Guide

The Lesson Pattern

This set of lessons is designed to aid *Bible study*, that is, to aid a consideration of the written Word of God, with discussion and personal application growing out of the text at hand.

The typical lesson is divided into these sections:

1. Theme Verse
2. Objectives
3. Questions and Answers
4. Closing

The theme verse and objectives give you, the leader, assistance in arousing the interest of the group in the concepts of the lesson. Focus on stimulating minds. Do not linger too long over the introductory remarks.

The questions and answers provide the real spadework necessary for Bible study. Here the class digs, uncovers, and discovers; it gets the facts and observes them. Comments from the leader are needed only to the extent that they help the group understand the text. The questions in this guide, corresponding to sections within the text, are intended to help the participants discover the meaning of the text.

Having determined what the text says, the class is ready to apply the message. Having heard, read, marked, and learned the Word of God, they can proceed to digest it inwardly through discussion, evaluation, and application. This is done, as this guide suggests, by taking the truths found in Scripture and applying them to the world, and Christianity in general, and then to one's personal Christian life. Class time may not permit discussion of all questions and topics. In preparation you may need to select one or two and focus on them. Close the session by reviewing one important truth from the lesson.

Remember, the Word of God is sacred, but this study guide is not. The notes in this section offer only guidelines and suggestions. Do not hesitate to alter the guidelines or substitute others to meet your needs and the needs of the participants. Adapt your teaching plan to your class and your class period.

Good teaching directs the learner to discover for himself or herself. For the teacher this means directing the learner, not giving the learner answers. Directing understanding takes preparation. Choose the verses that should be looked up in Scripture ahead of time. What discussion questions will you ask? At what points? Write them in the margin of your study guide. Involve class members, but give them clear directions. What practical actions might you propose for the week following the lesson? Which of the items do you consider most important for your class?

Consider how you can best use your teaching period. Do you have 45 minutes? An hour? Or an hour and a half? If time is short, what should you cut? Learn to become a wise steward of class time.

Plan a brief opening devotion, using members of the class. And be sure to take time to summarize the lesson, or have a class member do it.

Remember to pray frequently for yourself and your class. May God the Holy Spirit bless your study and your leading of others into the comforting truths of God's Christ-centered Word.

Lesson 1

Obadiah: Servant of the Lord

Theme verse: *Deliverers will go up on Mount Zion to govern the mountains of Esau. And the kingdom will be the LORD's.*

Obadiah 21

Objectives

By the power of the Holy Spirit working through God's Word, we will

- learn to appreciate Obadiah's little book, in spite of its size and apparent difficulties;
- recognize Obadiah's promise was ultimately fulfilled in Christ;
- grow in our confidence of God's faithfulness in the midst of our difficulties.

1. Portions of Obadiah and Jeremiah are remarkably similar. Yet, portions of the Gospels are remarkably similar, if not identical (for an example of the latter, compare Matthew 10:22; Mark 13:13; Luke 21:17). Luke records the process by which he obtained the material he provides in his Gospel: he accumulated eyewitness testimony. Regardless of the sources or processes used by Scripture writers, what they have written is God's inspired and inerrant Word, which "cannot deceive" (Luther, *Large Catechism*).

2. In addition to receiving a "vision" from God, the Bible uses various phrases—including "the word of the LORD came to"—to indicate that the prophets' words were not simply their own. There are many details about the Scriptures, which we may never know this side of heaven. Our trust, however, is not in knowing all the details, but in the reliability of God's Word.

3. Jesus, Paul, and Peter confirm that the Holy Spirit inspired the writers of the Scriptures so that every word in the Bible is the Word of God.

4. Adam and Eve's hearts were filled with deception when they doubted God's clear Word concerning the tree (Genesis 3:1). They desired knowledge to make them "like" Him (3:5). In relying on their own wisdom, Edom desired to be among the "stars" of the nations. This eerily reflects Satan's desire to exalt himself over God. These examples in the Bible clearly illustrate the results of sinful pride.

5. True and reliable wisdom comes from God alone. Apart from God's grace in the Word, people cannot establish a relationship with God. Those who try to do so are truly "foolish." On the cross of Christ God placards His wisdom (1 Corinthians 1:18–2:5), which is revealed to His children through Word and Sacrament, and apprehended by the gift of faith.

6. This portion of Obadiah tailors nicely with the psalm. Verse 7c refers to Jesus Christ, who quotes the psalm, and finds its fulfillment in His words and deeds at the Last Supper.

Both Zechariah and Paul (in 1 Corinthians) speak to the "day of the LORD" in terms of a joyous deliverance of those who trust in the Lord's promises, and of the graphic horrors for those spurning His Son. Both passages clearly announce the arrival of Jesus Christ on the Last Day, the "day of the LORD."

7. Both passages refer to the arrival of the ultimate Deliverer, Jesus Christ, and the close of history as we know it.

Christ our Lord will reign forever with His saints. Hebrews 12 provides a glimpse into the future heavenly Jerusalem. In the Lord's Supper, we take part in the blessings of Mount Zion by receiving a Eucharistic "foretaste" of the coming feast: the wedding supper of the Lamb (Revelation 19:9; 21:1–7; 22:1–6).

Answers may vary.

Lesson 2

Reluctant Missionary

Theme verse: *But the* L*ORD provided a great fish to swallow Jonah, and Jonah was inside the fish three days and three nights.*

Jonah 1:17

Objectives

By the power of the Holy Spirit working through God's Word, we will:

- understand the difference in calls between called church workers and individual Christians;
- grow in our appreciation and thankfulness for God's love for all people regardless of race or nationality;
- understand the reliability of Jonah's experience as historical truth;
- speak of God's mercy in Christ to our family, friends, and neighbors

Because of the great wealth of material for discussion, the teacher may need to devote more than one class period to this chapter. More time will probably have to be given to this first chapter than to any of the remaining chapters. Each section offers opportunity for discussing points of great practical value.

A good map showing the location of Nineveh should be at hand. According to Genesis 10:8–11, Nimrod was the founder of Nineveh (Micah 5:6). The ancients regarded some other cities in the neighborhood as parts of Nineveh. Therefore they always spoke of it as "a great city." (See Genesis 10:12; Jonah 1:2; 3:2–3.) Nothing is known of its early history. It came into prominence as the capital of Assyria during the struggles of that country with Babylon for world supremacy. In 612 B.C. (or 606, according to some scholars), Nineveh was captured and destroyed by the Babylonians.

8. The prophets and apostles were called immediately, that is, directly, by the Lord. God calls all who serve in the New Testament church as pastors, teachers, and missionaries, mediately through a Christian congregation or group of congregations (synod). These workers are specially prepared and commissioned to devote all their time to the Gospel ministry. On the other hand, by virtue of their Baptism, all Christians are called to spread the Gospel at home and abroad, by personal testimony or evangelism, and by supporting the work of the church with their prayers and earthly means. (See Galatians 3:26–29; Philippians 1:3–6; Colossians 3:15–17; 1 Thessalonians 1:4–10; 1 Peter 2:4–10.)

9. The text gives the impression that Jonah rushed to Joppa with all possible speed. Here he found what he was looking for: a chance to go to the extreme western end of the known world. The Phoenicians carried on a regular trade on the Mediterranean between Asia and the colonies they had planted in North Africa (Carthage) and Spain (Tartessus). Using a map, note the length of the journey to Spain.

Jonah's thoughts were probably these: If I do not go to Nineveh, God's punishment will overtake the wicked city; but if I preach to them, God might still have mercy upon them and spare them. Therefore, I will flee and leave these enemies of my people to their well-deserved fate.

Jonah's sin was not the sin of gross unbelief, but of disobedience and of refusing to acknowledge God as the God of grace. He was willing to go among the Ninevites and be served by them, but he would do nothing to save their souls. Jonah's narrow, perverted view of God and of His will made him selfish and stubborn.

10. Luther says God is present in two ways: In a natural and physical sense He is present everywhere, but spiritually to the soul He is present only where He reveals Himself by His Word. In Israel the Lord revealed Himself to His people, but since Jonah did not regard Him also as the God of the Gentiles, he believed that among them he would be outside the range of God's communications to men. That Jonah was at home in the Psalms, and must therefore have known Psalm 139, is evident from his prayer in chapter 2.

Answers will vary.

11. During the winter months severe storms were common on the Mediterranean and made shipping dangerous. It was at such a time that St. Paul, against his will, made his perilous journey that ended in shipwreck. Shipping was usually suspended during the stormy winter season. Hence Jonah's trip was evidently made in summer, for the sailors did not expect such a storm and found it to be worse than anything they had experienced. Paul, of course, could make his trip with a good conscience and even received the assurance from the Lord that he would reach his destination, Rome. But contrary to Paul, Jonah had no business on the ship he had boarded.

Many Bible commentators have written about Jonah's sleeping on the ship. He, indeed, may have been tired, as Jesus was on the Sea of Galilee, but there the parallel ends. Jonah's sleep is likened to the sleep of sin. He probably hoped that by sleeping away the time he could banish all thoughts of God and silence his accusing conscience.

12. Every sailor on the boat prayed to some god when death in the waves seemed inevitable. There are many examples on record of people who learned to pray during times of grave, personal crisis such as war, severe illness, and so forth. It is, however, surprising that Jonah, a man who should have been a man of prayer, did not pray. Perhaps his conscience told him that God would not hear him because of his sin. In this situation Jonah is a type of the "Christian" who neglects prayer.

Answers will vary.

13. The unbelieving sailors revealed that they had a natural knowledge and fear of God (see Romans 1:20–23). Their consciences were not dulled and hardened, and they wanted to do what was right. They gave Jonah an opportunity to defend himself and state his case. They did not wish to decide on the manner of atonement for the crime nor lay their hands on him. They did not want to kill a man who had done them no harm or sacrifice him to their own advantage.

Jonah is a type of Christ in so far as he voluntarily offered to die in order that others might be saved. Jonah, however, was suffering for his own sins. The prophet who did not want to preach to the unbelievers at Nineveh had to preach to unbelievers on the ship. The sudden calming of the sea proved to the sailors the power of Jonah's God (Matthew 8:27). We are not told whether these men were truly converted and remained faithful worshipers of the Lord. We may assume that at least some of them became true believers.

14. Coming now to the story of Jonah and the fish, the teacher may spend some time to discuss the plausibility. Although the Christian acknowledges, on the basis of Scripture alone, the fact that God here performed a great miracle, it is nevertheless satisfying to learn that such events with God's intervention are entirely possible.

The original Hebrew text says nothing about a whale, but uses the word *dag,* which may mean any large fish or sea creature. The same is true of the Greek word *ketos* in Matthew 12:40. We are not told what kind of fish this was. It may have been a whale; there are many species of whales, some of which do have an immense throat cavity (e.g., killer whales) capable of swallowing large animals. But this fish may also have been a shark, or some sea creature now extinct. A number of cases have been reported of men who had been swallowed by large sea creatures and who were brought forth alive again after these fish had been caught. We are not to understand "provided" (v. 17) as meaning that God at this moment created a special fish. God merely directed this fish to go to the place where Jonah was in the water and to take him into its stomach, in order to preserve him from drowning. To the believer the whole thing is wonderfully miraculous.

Jonah's stay in the fish is typical of Christ's death and resurrection (Matthew 12:40). The Hebrews counted any part of a day as a whole day. Jonah may not have remained in the fish for 72 hours, just as Jesus did not remain in the grave for that length of time (Friday night regarded as one day; Saturday as one day; early Sunday morning as the third day). It was indeed a strange way in which God preserved His prophet from death, but the Bible and history are full of divine miracles of preservation. Jonah's imprisonment within the fish was a unique and terrible experience for him, but it effectively taught him that God was merciful in spite of his disobedience. Christians are comforted by God's Word, which teaches that God is present everywhere, and through Christ, blesses us in every circumstance (Psalm 139:9–11).

Lesson 3

Prayer and Deliverance

Theme verse: *And the LORD commanded the fish, and it vomited Jonah onto dry land.*

Jonah 2:10

Objectives

By the power of the Holy Spirit working through God's Word, we will:

- rediscover that God hears and answers prayers in all situations;
- learn that God's discipline can lead to repentance and faith;
- offer praise and thanksgiving to our gracious Savior.

Jonah's prayer in the belly of the fish proves, if a proof is necessary at all, the truth of the story of Jonah. Nowhere in secular literature do we find a prayer that could be compared with that of Jonah. Only a believer in the true God could have prayed as he prayed. This prayer was spoken and written by a prophet who was inspired by the Spirit of God in the same degree as were the authors of the psalms.

15. We are not told that Jonah prayed during the storm. But when he was in the fish, he prayed fervently and in a God-pleasing manner. Hence we must conclude that he had repented of his sin and that God had revived his faith. For only a believer can truly pray and worship God. The Lord had accomplished His purpose with respect to Jonah when He brought His disobedient prophet into great tribulation. In the school of affliction Jonah learned to pray and to make proper use of God's Word. As someone said, the belly of the fish became for Jonah a seminary in which he learned practical theology. Jonah was certainly in as uncomfortable a position as any human being ever found himself

(darkness, stifling air, nauseating odors). Fortunately, a child of God may pray anywhere, for God is omnipresent.

Answers may vary.

16. People who have come face-to-face with death have related that their whole life suddenly flashed before their minds, and that they remembered sins they had long forgotten. The heaping of words used by Jonah to describe the sea shows how terrifying the sea had suddenly become when he felt himself sinking into its depths.

However, Jonah recognized God's discipline, and humbled himself in repentance. Despite his hopeless situation, Jonah would not let go of God. He thought of God's gracious presence in His temple and eagerly reached out to receive the grace which God there offered. In his extremity Jonah reminds us of Job. (See Job 13:15; 19:25–27.)

No evil, including drowning, can extinguish the hope of a believer (Psalms 42:11; 37:5; 46:1–5). The world knows nothing of this hope, which is even stronger than the fear of death.

17. Jonah learned from experience that nothing is of such great value to man as to possess faith in God. There is, of course, much more to such a faith than merely believing that there is a God (James 2:19). He alone has real faith who regards God as his own personal God. Note that Jonah addressed the Lord as "my" God. He now thinks of his God only as a gracious, loving, and saving God.

What caused faith to be revived and sustained in Jonah? "I remembered You, LORD." All that he had learned and knew about the Lord suddenly became alive in his mind. We may well take it that he then thought of those beautiful passages in the Psalms which he knew from memory and which he embodied in his prayer. Through the Word of God that spoke to him in his heart, Jonah had again found his God. Where He is with His grace, there is heaven and salvation.

Discuss Scripture references.

18. Motivated by the Lord's salvation, Christians naturally offer sacrifices of praise and thanksgiving. These may take on various forms. Jonah ends his prayer in harmonious cadences of heartfelt gratitude. Here he makes a definite promise to God. The sacrifice he will bring to Him is a song of praise and thanksgiving; this very hymn which he later wrote down shows that he kept his promise.

Regarding Jonah's vow, Luther is right in believing that this refers only to the prophet's promise to praise and serve God, to consecrate his life to Him. It was the same kind of vow that we made at our Baptism and renewed at our confirmation.

Jonah may, however, also have had in mind that special work which God had commanded him to do and which he is now willing to perform, if God is still willing to send him.

Answers may vary.

Lesson 4

Missionary Success

Theme verse: *When God saw what they did and how they turned from their evil ways, He had compassion and did not bring upon them the destruction He had threatened.*

Jonah 3:10

Objectives

By the power of the Holy Spirit working through God's Word, we will:

- understand the importance of faithfully supporting our missionaries and efforts to share the Gospel;
- learn that Christian repentance involves a change of heart and faith, which expresses itself in the fruits of faith;
- share the Good News of God's compassion in Christ with a friend or family member this week.

With chapter 3 the story of Jonah, so to speak, begins all over again. It opens with the same command of God to His prophet as did chapter 1. Yet, there is a great difference between these two chapters. God is still the same, but not Jonah. He had learned the futility of trying to disobey the Lord. Though he is not yet convinced that God's prophet should preach to Gentiles, he knows that he must go to wherever his Lord sends him. He has learned that a servant of God does not follow his or her own will, but he or she follows the will of the heavenly Master. Jonah's lesson applies not only to pastors, teachers, and missionaries, but also to each individual Christian.

19. God kept calling Jonah until he went. Likewise He keeps calling the members of His church to do mission work, individually and collectively, in the community and at distant places, as often as He brings the spiritual needs of others to their attention (through church papers, reports of missionaries, requests like Acts 16:9). Jonah's

responsibility should remind us individually of our missionary obligations. If Jonah had not gone to Nineveh, that city with its large population would have perished. Countless unbelievers would have died in their sins.

If Christians would more liberally supply the church today with the necessary means, many additional missionaries could be placed in the mission fields. In order to obtain the needed number of workers, many more than we have at present should be willing to say, "Here am I, send me" (Isaiah 6:8).

Every one of these must be willing and able to preach and teach the Word just as God wants it preached—not adding any of his or her own wisdom (1 Peter 4:11).

20. Subduing all self-will and following divine instructions, Jonah obeyed the word of the Lord. Such obedience to a divine command should be observed by all Christians, especially by all preachers and teachers. Our pastors and missionaries have been called into their work by the Lord through the church, and thus they, too, have received their instructions from on high. The Bible tells them what they are to preach and teach; it also assures them that their work will not be in vain (Isaiah 55:11).

Jonah probably did all his preaching in the streets and marketplaces of Nineveh. Paul did the same thing in Athens (Acts 17:17–33). However, it was the usual practice of the apostles to do their public preaching in synagogues or other available buildings.

Jonah seems to have preached only the Law (as far as the text indicates), but he certainly told the Ninevites about the Lord and at least incidentally sowed seeds of the Gospel, otherwise they could not have believed (v. 5).

God has entrusted us Christians with the message of repentance of sins, and faith in Christ crucified and resurrected. The goal of this message is not a "decision for Christ," but always the Sacrament of Holy Baptism, which brings forgiveness, life, and salvation (see Acts 2:37–41; 8:34–38; 9:17–19; 10:46–48; 16:14–15, 29–34; 18:7–8; 19:1–7; 22:12–16).

21. The question about the sincerity of the Ninevites' repentance is definitely settled by Christ in Luke 11:32. Jesus used the New Testament term for repentance, which means a complete change of heart. Only true believers would be able to rise on the Last Day as witnesses against the generations of Christ's time.

Jonah 3:5 says explicitly that the people of Nineveh "believed" God ("Yahweh," the true God). In verse 9 the original Hebrew text has the phrase "*the* God"; this can refer only to the God whom Jonah had preached. Note that it is nowhere said that the people called upon their idols. Apparently they had abandoned their gods and in their distress called upon the Lord alone.

The Ninevites furnished proof for their repentance by their actions. Middle Easterners used these rites not only to display their grief, but also to show sorrow over their sins (1 Kings 21:27). God has neither commanded nor forbidden such ceremonies. These externals have no value in themselves (Joel 2:12–13). But if they are the expression of contrite hearts, they serve a good purpose. This was the case with the Ninevites, for in verse 8, prayer and turning from sin are stressed as the main thing. These things God saw as the fruits of faith, and they moved Him to spare the city (v. 10).

In times of trouble we should pray to God for deliverance, but we may do this only conditionally ("if it be Your will"). God may not answer our prayer as we would like to have it answered; He may answer it in some other and better way.

22. This verse contains two important matters that need to be discussed. First, "God saw what they did." This passage furnishes no ground for teaching that people, even unbelievers, can make themselves acceptable to God and merit His grace by good works. God looked upon the works, the change of conduct of the Ninevites, as fruits of their faith (v. 5). They would not have done what they did if they had not believed in God. This text fully agrees with the central doctrine of the Bible that the justification of the sinner is by faith only, as Luther shows convincingly in his exposition of the Book of Jonah. Christ refers to our good works as evidences of our faith (Matthew 25:34–46). God did not destroy Ninevah solely due to His grace.

23. Discuss these two points briefly, especially in the light of Luke 11:32. The people of Nineveh repented after hearing the prophet Jonah, who had no love for them. We have more than Jonah. We have the full Gospel of Christ. Every preacher of the New Testament is more than Jonah because he has the whole Word of God. The Lord has given much more to us than to Nineveh. He wants us to share our blessings with all mankind. God grant that the people of Nineveh may not rise up against us on the Last Day!

Lesson 5

Prejudice and Rebuke

Theme verse: *But Nineveh has more than a hundred and twenty thousand people who cannot tell their right hand from their left, and many cattle as well. Should I not be concerned about that great city?*

Jonah 4:11

Objectives

By the power of the Holy Spirit working through God's Word, we will:

- understand that God's compassion through Christ extends to all people, regardless of race, color, or nationality;
- grow in our appreciation of God's mercy;
- tell others of God's love, grace, and comfort to His dear children.

In this fourth chapter, the story of Jonah reaches its climax. We do not believe that Jonah's obstinacy is impossible since we have the same human heart that Jonah had (Jeremiah 17:9). Thus Jonah's heart isn't the only one described here. Rather, by Jonah's example, God portrays to our eyes the natural disposition of our own hearts. He does so in such glaring colors "that we may learn to look with terror at our sins and to regard them as great indeed and to find joy and comfort in Christ alone and thus be saved through such faith" (Luther).

24. Jonah expressed his extreme displeasure with God by means of a prayer. In it he accused God of something with which no sinful mortal should ever think of finding fault. Jonah was thoroughly familiar with the books of Moses, and he quoted correctly from Exodus 34:6. This sweet Gospel message suited Jonah only in so far as it was applied to him and his nation, but it was most offensive to him inasmuch as it applied also to the Gentiles. There are still some members of Christian churches who would become furious if they saw

persons unlike them in race or color worshiping in their sanctuaries. Have we ever committed this sin of Jonah?

Although it was a grievous sin that Jonah quarreled with God, the Lord does not treat him as an enemy, but as a friend. He does not reprove him as an ungodly person, but patiently corrects him as a child, only asking him a question (v. 4). What fatherly, tender, boundless love and mercy He bestows upon His erring servant! The Book of Jonah teaches also this lesson: whoever is saved is saved by divine grace alone.

25. Jonah may have built his hut on the top of one of the high hills that overlook Nineveh, from which he had a good view of the city. God seemingly approved of his "vacationing" at that spot when He provided the prophet with special comforts, but it was not Jonah's personal interests that moved Him to provide the vine. This special gift of God was to "ease his discomfort." By "discomfort" is not meant the oppressive heat of the sun, but rather his resentment because of God's dealing with Nineveh. Jonah was to regard this lovely shade, provided miraculously for his benefit, as a token of God's loving-kindness. Thus God seeks to make us forget our griefs and annoyances by granting us all kinds of little joys and pleasures. These comforts are means in God's hands to help us, His children, over the rough places in our daily pilgrimage; they are precious tokens of His love, which He bestows upon us (Psalm 111:2).

26. The Lord now showed Jonah that he was inconsistent and unreasonable. Jonah, motivated by his selfishness, had felt sorry for the insignificant vine, yet he was angry that God had spared a city with a large number of people whose immortal souls were worth far more than a short-lived plant. Consider what Christ says about the value of a soul (see Mark 8:36–37; Luke 15:10).

The Lord clearly indicates to Jonah and to all the Jews that He desires the salvation of all people, including the Gentiles. But the Jews never learned that lesson. Note how difficult it was for the apostles and first Christians to learn this truth (Acts 10 and 11). Wherever Christians reveal prejudice against any race, nationality, or person, they prove that they, too, have not learned this lesson as yet.

Note the abrupt manner in which the Book of Jonah closes. Nothing more needed to be said. Jonah had now learned his lesson. When he later wrote his book, he told the story, as we have it, in order that it might serve as a frank confession of his own sins and a glorious testimony to the universal grace of God. Another lesson this book teaches is that God shows infinite patience in dealing with His weak and erring children. For that reason this book is most comforting to us.

Answers will vary.

Lesson 6

Micah: Preacher of Promise

Theme Verse: *Look! The* L*ORD is coming from His dwelling place; He comes down and treads the high places of the earth.*

Micah 1:3

Objectives

By the power of the Holy Spirit working through God's Word, we will:

- reflect on how God uses the forces of nature to draw our attention toward repentance;
- discuss how we might prepare ourselves for the Lord's coming on the Last Day.

Chapters 1 and 2 contain the message of Micah's first address. After a general announcement of judgment on account of the sins of Israel (1:2–5), Micah predicts the destruction of Samaria (vv. 6–7) and the devastation of Judah with the deportation of its inhabitants (vv. 6–16). He justifies this threat by an earnest reproof of the many acts of injustice and violence on the part of the upper classes (2:1–5), and a severe condemnation of the false prophets who misled the people (2:6–11). His first address closes with the Gospel assurance that the believing "remnant" in Israel will, with all believers from among the Gentiles, form the blessed flock of Christ, the Good Shepherd (2:12–13). Micah's first sermon is, therefore, primarily a stern preaching of the Law, which warns and threatens the sinner with divine punishment. Nevertheless, it is noteworthy that Micah closes his fierce denunciation of sin with a sweet Gospel note for the benefit of all who take his message to heart.

27. The prophet describes the terrors which attend the Lord's coming in judgment (Psalm 18). God often uses the forces of nature (earthquakes, fire, storms, floods) to carry out His judgments. Puny

man is helpless before Him who can tear the mountains apart, melt the earth, and sweep everything into the sea. The similes, "like wax," "like water," express the utter helplessness of man and of all creatures before God's almighty power to destroy. (Wax melts away and water cannot stand in its downward fall, but is diffused. See Psalm 97:5; Isaiah 64:1–3.)

In such a manner, as described, the Lord is about to execute judgment upon the nations of Israel and Judah. The reason why God's wrath against them has been stirred to the utmost is their apostasy, their sins of idolatry and wickedness, which cry to high heaven for punishment. All Israel is guilty, the whole of the covenant nation.

Micah's warning fits our day, since the world is certainly ripe for judgment. The recent experiences of war and unrest have proved that consequences to actions can be terrible. But, like the Israelites and Judahites of Micah's time, many today also have failed to take the warnings to heart. As Christians, we should be thinking and talking more about Judgment Day and hold ourselves in constant readiness for it.

28. Special attention needs to be given to the figurative language and poetic imagery with which this section is replete. Micah seeks by means of figurative speech to stimulate the thinking of his people in the right direction and to touch their hearts more effectively.

Micah here speaks not in his own name, but in the name of his nation. Hence, he describes himself in the costume of a prisoner, not that of a mourner. His intention was to set forth in a symbolical form the fate that awaited the Judeans. They would be stripped of all their prosperity and glory.

The penetration of the judgment into Judah is now depicted by a reference to cities which will be smitten. Micah plays on the meaning the names of these cities have in Hebrew. The first sentence of verse 10 is borrowed from 2 Samuel 1:20. The Philistines are not to hear of the distress of Judah, lest they should rejoice over it. Micah then mentions ten places in which Judah will experience something very painful (ten, the number of completeness). The names of these places, with slight alterations, depicted what would take place within them. He notes that the enemy will approach from the north. Ophrah was near Bethel (Joshua 18:23). To roll in the dust marked deep sorrow. The inhabitants of Saphir, a beautiful city north of Jerusalem, would go into captivity. Zanaan, or Zenan (Joshua 15:37), seems to mean "come forth," but in reality it did not come forth to fight. Beth-ezel, near Jerusalem, may mean "Near House"; the calamity will not stop near it, as one would expect from its name, but spread to other cities. This name has been interpreted variously; what it means is not clear. Maroth was apparently in the neighborhood of Jerusalem. It is described as writhing in pain, it was probably plundered by Sennacherib's army on his way to Jerusalem. Maroth's bitter grief is on account of the good which it lost.

The judgment will spread over wide areas of Judah. Lachish was a fortified city in the plain; here Sennacherib fixed his headquarters (2 Kings 18:14, 17). This was the first city of Judah, according to this passage, to introduce the worship of the idols of the Northern Kingdom. Upon this city judgment would fall with great severity, because it had given offense and led others into sin. From Lachish idolatry spread to Jerusalem. Moresheth-gath Judah was compelled to yield to the foe. Achzib, a city in the plain of Judah, would live up to its name and deceive the expectation of the nation. Mareshah would no longer be an inheritance of Judah but would fall into other hands. "I will bring a conqueror against you," that is, the Assyrian (Micah 1:15). Adullam is called the glory of Israel, because of its secure position; when it fell, Israel's glory was gone. Micah mentions Adullam simply on account of the cave there (1 Samuel 22:1), which might serve the nobility of Judah as a last place of refuge.

Lesson 7

The Coming King

Theme verse: *I will surely gather all of you, O Jacob; I will surely bring together the remnant of Israel . . . Their king will pass through before them, the* L*ORD of their head.*

Micah 2:12–13

Objectives

By the power of the Holy Spirit working through God's Word, we will:

- learn more about the great evils of covetousness and oppression;
- grow in appreciating true prophets who preach and teach only God's Word;
- rejoice in the comfort and care of our Good Shepherd, Jesus Christ.

After having prophesied in chapter 1 of the judgment that would fall upon both kingdoms on account of their apostasy from the Lord, Micah proceeds in chapter 2 to denounce the prevalent social evils, the insatiable greed and the revolting acts of injustice and violence, which had made the nations ripe for judgment (vv. 1–5). He then vindicates his threat, as opposed to the prophecies of the false prophets, who confirmed the nation in its ungodliness by the lies that they told (vv. 6–11). He brings his first sermon to a close with a brief but definite promise that the Messiah would, during the time of His reign as King, gather together the remnant of Israel (all believers from among the Jews and Gentiles), bring them into the fold of His church, give them victory over all their enemies, and lead them safely through all uncertainties of life into His heavenly kingdom (vv. 12–13).

29. Note that Micah dealt with the hypocritical, self-righteous, and ungodly of his day very much in the same manner as did Jesus in

Matthew 23:13–37. Micah's denunciation applied to the great and mighty of the nation, who by acts of injustice deprived the common people of the inheritance conferred upon them by the Lord (Isaiah 5:8). He describes the evils that undermine the welfare of society and destroy a nation: shrewd schemes for personal gain (v. 1); heartless oppression of the poor (v. 2); covetousness (v. 3). Discuss how these evils are prevalent today in our own country.

The Bible describes covetousness, or greed, in the most unfavorable of terms. The desire to possess what one does not have acts as a concern and eats away at one's happiness and peace. It destroys relationships, eventually even one's relationship with God.

30. The Israelites took great pride in calling themselves "the house of Jacob" (v. 7), but how unlike the godly patriarch they were in their attitude toward God's Word! The leaders mock Micah, strengthened in their position by the false prophets. They did not like his preaching. Therefore God abandons them to their own ways. He takes them at their word and fits the punishment to their sin. (See Isaiah 30:10; Amos 2:12; 7:16; 2 Timothy 4:3.) Micah was an uncompromising preacher, who would not yield to the masses or conform to the preaching of the more popular false prophets. Note his unflinching testimony to God's holiness, righteousness, and justice (v. 7).

This prophecy of Micah was, of course, far different from what the false prophets were promising the people and hence most unwelcome to them (v. 11). Micah's remarks about the false prophets lying and deceiving when they predicted great prosperity and a pleasant life of luxury sound like bitter sarcasm.

Here, again, it should be easy to make the application to modern conditions, as suggested by the questions for discussion. Answers may vary.

31. Here we have Micah's first reference to the Messiah. This passage comes as a refreshing sequel, for the believers, to Micah's fierce denunciation of sin. His predictions of judgments would cause sincere hearts to tremble, and they might ask: What will become of the chosen race from whom the Messiah is to descend? To comfort them, Micah tells them what the Messiah will do for them. We need not worry that the church will ever perish, no matter how much Satan rages against it (Matthew 16:18). The Messiah will seek out all His sheep and bring them into His flock, the church, in which He will provide

them with all they need, as Psalm 23 teaches. Verse 12a refers neither to all Jews nor to the return from Babylon, for that restoration was only partial. The "all of you" are "the remnant of Israel," the true spiritual Israel, of which all Gentile believers are also a part. (See Romans 11:25–26; 9:6–33; Isaiah 10:20–22.) "Multitude of men" points to the conversion of the Gentiles (John 10:16).

Answers may vary.

Lesson 8

False Prophets Rejected

Theme Verse: *As for the prophets who lead My people astray, if one feeds them, they proclaim "peace"; if he does not, they prepare to wage war against him.*

Micah 3:5

Objectives

By the power of the Holy Spirit working through God's Word, we will:

- learn how God expects earthly rulers to rule justly;
- understand the authority of our pastors when they speak God's Word to us;
- give thanks for God's faithfulness in fulfilling His prophecies made by His prophets.

Micah's second address (chapters 3–5) is of a predominantly messianic character. This address opens in chapter 3 with the announcement of the exile of the people and the destruction of Jerusalem on account of the corruption of both the civil rulers and the spiritual leaders of the nation. This serves to prepare the way for the prophecy which follows in chapters 4 and 5, the promise of the salvation with which the remnant of Israel, that has been preserved throughout the judgment, will be blessed in the future. The threat of punishment, in chapter 3, is specially directed against the leaders of Israel.

32. In this first section the ruling classes are denounced. It could not be said that their conduct in office represented the kind of government that God wants to have administered on earth (Romans 13:3–4). By them the idea that "rulers are not a terror to good works, but to the evil" was reversed. It was their duty to give heed to what was

right and just. That is the special function of government (1 Timothy 2:2).

They should also have known that God will judge unjust rulers. But they were rulers such as Solomon condemned in his Book of Proverbs (e.g., Proverbs 17:25; 24:23–24; 28:15; 29:2). "Hating good and loving evil" characterizes these men as being a curse to their nation. Instead of administering justice to the people, they took off their skin and tore the flesh from their bones. (See Psalm 14:4; Proverbs 30:14).

Verse 4 contains God's judgment upon these sinners (Proverbs 1:24–32). Micah harks back to 2:3. In 7:2–5 he again takes up this indictment of the ruling classes. It is bad enough when God will not listen to the cries of the distressed, but it is much worse when He hides His face from them, for that means that He has completely withdrawn His mercy from them and has utterly forsaken them. Men cannot do evil and expect to fare well. (See Luke 23:41a; James 2:13.) God's judgments answer to men's evil doings.

33. Micah describes the false prophets as men who predict peace and prosperity for a morsel of bread and thereby lead the people astray, setting before them earthly prosperity instead of preaching repentance and obedience to God's Word. Thus they became accomplices of the wicked rulers, who used them to their benefit. Whoever gave them a sufficient amount of bribe money or rewarded them with nice gifts, was sure to obtain the kind of preaching he liked to hear. But for those who gave them nothing they had only doleful predictions of evil. Sanctimoniously they would refer to such misfortunes as just and holy judgments of God.

Eventually the falsehood spoken by false prophets will catch up with them. Salvation and prosperity will be denied to them. They will be disgraced, because their false prophecies will be exposed as lies.

In verse 8 Micah contrasts himself with the false prophets, as being full of the power of the Spirit. He has the firm conviction that he is speaking the truth of God. This is neither the boast of an egotist nor pharisaical self-righteousness. Rather, it is the confident declaration of his own spiritual experience and assurance. His authority, and a pastor's authority, comes from the fact that God speaks through them when they speak God's Word.

34. Here begins the leading subject of Micah's prophecy: a demonstration of his assertion that he is "filled with power, with the

Spirit of the LORD" (v. 8). He announces the threat of punishment for which the way has been prepared by verses 2–7. To this end, he once more sums up the sins of which the leaders are guilty. The civil rulers are addressed in verses 9–10; the priests and prophets included in verse 11. These are charged with the crimes of cruel extortion, slave labor, injustice, bribery, and witchcraft. They claimed immunity for themselves on the grounds that they were God's people. They never reflected that the Lord demands sanctification of life and punishes sin.

Micah is apparently the first prophet to prophesy definitively the destruction of Jerusalem (v. 12). When Jeremiah did the same thing years later, he was accused of treason (Jeremiah 26). Fortunately, some of the princes then remembered this prophecy of Micah and excused Jeremiah on the grounds that Hezekiah had taken no action against Micah (Jeremiah 26:18). "Zion" here is the hill on which stood the royal palace; "Jerusalem" refers to the rest of the city; the temple hill (Mount Moriah—"mountain of the house") is also mentioned for the purpose of destroying all false trust in the temple (Jeremiah 7:4). The fulfillment of this threat is more definitely described in Micah 4:10. Jerusalem, which the Jews believed God would never give over to an enemy, was destroyed by the Babylonians in 586 B.C., in A.D. 70 by the Romans, and several times later. To this day it has remained a chief trouble spot in the world. Yet, as the next chapter indicates, it has played a more important part in the history of the human race than any other city.

Lesson 9

The Lord's Mountain

Theme verse: *Come, let us go up to the mountain of the* LORD, *to the house of the God of Jacob. He will teach us His ways, so that we may walk in His paths.*

Micah 4:2

Objectives

By the power of the Holy Spirit working through God's Word, we will:

- understand the term, "the mountain of the LORD's temple," as referring figuratively to the church;
- give thanks for the ultimate victory of the church over her enemies.

This is Micah's great mercy chapter, which comes in the very middle of his book. We observe here a great change in tone. The Lord, who pronounced such severe judgments upon Israel, suddenly turns to comfort His people with the prospect of coming glories and with the assurance of final deliverance and victory. Remarkably, both Isaiah and Micah paint the same picture of the church in almost identical words. We need not be concerned about the question whether Micah copied from Isaiah or vice versa. Both men penned the same words by divine inspiration. That is all we can say.

35. "The mountain of the LORD's temple" (4:1) is an expression used typically of the church, as is "kingdom of heaven" (Matthew 13:31–32). It represents the ideal Zion, which under Christ was to be elevated to its greatest importance and dignity. The temple mountain was regarded as the seat of God's rule, from which the Law was proclaimed. The exaltation ascribed to it is not of a physical, but of a spiritual nature. "Raised above the hills" means visible before the eyes of all men. These descriptions cannot be applied to any locality.

"Peoples will stream to it" (Isaiah says "all nations") points to the universal extent of the church and to the conversion of the Gentiles (Psalm 100; Isaiah 60).

The nations are represented as seeking to know the true God. In reality, God is leading them into the church by having its missionaries preach the Gospel to them (Matthew 28:18–20). The church is the place where salvation is preached. Hence "mountain" (v. 2) is not thought of as a place of worship, but as the place where God reveals Himself through His Word, Law and Gospel. In the New Testament era the church will consist of "many nations" in contrast with the one nation, Israel, in the Old Testament. The believers in all these nations will willingly submit to the rule of God's Word, as verses 3–5 indicate.

36. The prophecies of Micah were not an attempt to end all wars upon earth and to proclaim an era of universal and perpetual peace (millennium). If that had been their intention, they would not only have proved themselves to have been idle dreams, but they would also have contradicted such clear teachings of Scripture as Matthew 24:7–21; Romans 3:10–18; James 4:1, and Joel 3:9–13. The world and the natural hearts of men will always remain the same, corrupt, full of hatred, greed, and revenge (Matthew 15:19).

Neither does the Bible deny to the governments of the nations the right to wield weapons and wage wars (see Luke 3:14; Romans 13:4). However, our text does not apply to civil governments, for the prophet is here solely talking about the church. In it there will always reign spiritual peace, because its Head and Ruler is our Peace (Ephesians 2:14).

37. "Watchtower of the flock" (v. 8) is here not the tower near Bethlehem (Genesis 35:21), but the tower of David's castle in Jerusalem. "Stronghold," or "hill" (*Ophel* in Hebrew) is an impregnable height on Mount Zion. (See 2 Chronicles 27:3; 33:14; Isaiah 32:14; Nehemiah 3:26–27.) Here the same place is viewed as a lookout point and a fort for watching and guarding the flock. "The Daughter of Zion" is the church personified as a virgin. The last two clauses of verse 8 are parallel and presuppose that Israel has lost the Davidic rule and kingdom. "The former dominion," the kingdom of Israel at its best under David and Solomon, was typical of the glory of the New Testament church. To His church God will give a dominion and glory greater than Israel ever had.

The last section (vv. 11–13) describes the conflict of the church with her enemies in the world. They fight against her to profane her, and they rejoice over her shame and sorrow (Micah 7:10). (See also Psalm 137; Lamentations 2:16; Obadiah 11–13.) But God will not forsake His own. God's counsel is to discipline His people for a time with the foe as a scourge and then to destroy the foe by the hands of others (Isaiah 55:8). The enemy is heaped up for destruction, as sheaves, in the Lord's judgment. Threshing was done by treading the grain with the feet (figurative for subduing the enemy, Isaiah 21:10). Verse 13 refers to the Middle Eastern custom of threshing out grain with oxen. The ox's strength lay in his horns. (See Deuteronomy 33:17; 1 Kings 22:11; Amos 6:13.) God will give His church strength to overcome the nations with the Gospel (Romans 15:12). God subjects the nations to Zion that these may serve His glory. (See Isaiah 60:6, 9; 23:18; Zechariah 14:20; Philippians 2:11.)

Lesson 10

The Saving Shepherd

Theme Verse: *But you, Bethlehem Ephrathah, though you are small among the clans of Judah, out of you will come for Me one who will be ruler over Israel, whose origins are from of old, from ancient times.*

Micah 5:2

Objectives

By the power of the Holy Spirit working through God's Word, we will:

- discover the importance of the timing, manner, and place of the Savior's birth;
- learn the Scripture's confirmation of the preexistence of God's Son;
- give thanks for Christ, our Shepherd and our Peace.

Classes studying this course during the fall quarter will come to this chapter in Micah shortly before the Christmas season. This will enable the leader to inject more of the Christmas spirit into the lesson and arouse a greater interest of the class participants in this messianic prophecy. In the study of this chapter the chief emphasis will naturally be placed on Micah's words pertaining to Bethlehem and the birth of Christ. This prophecy should be carefully compared with the fulfillment, as recorded in Matthew 2 and Luke 2. The other sections of this chapter may be covered more rapidly, giving only enough attention to detail to help the class participants grasp the sense and see how the Messiah's office and work, particularly in His present state of exaltation, are sketched by Micah in broad outline.

38. Verse 1 indicates that the Messiah would come after Judah had been degraded as a nation. "Israel's ruler," the Davidic line of kings, had fallen.

In 37 B.C. Herod the Idumean, a descendant of Esau, captured Jerusalem and, with the help of Rome, established himself in Judea as king.

Nevertheless, from that Davidic line would arise a King whose kingdom would last forever and ever.

39. Rachel was buried near Bethlehem (Genesis 35:19); Ruth became an ancestress of David in Bethlehem (Ruth 1:19; 4:11); and David lived and was anointed king in Bethlehem (1 Samuel 17:12).

Just as He takes a young girl and makes her the mother of His Son, so, too, does God take a small village to be the seat of David's royal house and the birthplace of the Messiah.

40. God says, literally, that the Messiah will rule, "for Me." God's glory is made the ultimate end of redemption here. Christ is to be the "Ruler over Israel." (See Genesis 49:10; 2 Samuel 23:3; Isaiah 11:1–4; Jeremiah 30:21.)

The phrase "whose origins are from of old" indicates the Messiah's preexistence. The passage ascribes the divine attributes of eternity to the Messiah who is both God and man in one person.

Verse 3 does not mention a human father, which hints at Christ's virgin birth. The role played by the Virgin Mary in Christ's birth was one of pure divine grace.

41. "He will stand" implies perseverance: His will be a permanent kingdom. Here we are shown the greatness and beneficence of His rule. His real work is to "shepherd" His flock. This term characterizes the Savior's reign. He feeds and nourishes souls with the Word. "Shepherd" includes rule. (See Isaiah 40:11; 49:10; Ezekiel 34:23.) He possesses the majesty of the Lord's attributes, hence is true God.

According to Christ's human nature the Lord is His God. The result of His rule for His people is the blessedness of peace. "His greatness" signifies both the exercise of superior power and its acknowledgment in humble submission by His subjects. He is great in the hearts of the believers. His church shall extend over the whole earth. "Peace" describes the effect of His redemption for all mankind (Hosea 2:18; Luke 2:14).

How Christ is our Peace is explained in the rest of the chapter: (1) by defending Israel against the attacks of its enemies (5b–6); (2) by exalting it into a power able to overcome the nations (7–9); (3) by exterminating everything that is contrary to the nature and life of the church (10–15).

The Messiah also endows His people with the power to overcome their enemies (vv. 7–8). The "remnant," the true believers (v. 3). "In the midst of the many peoples," that is, the church will come upon many nations like a refreshing dew from the Lord and will produce new life among them. (See Psalm 110:3; Hosea 14:5; Psalm 72:6.) "Which do not wait for man"—the conversion of sinners is entirely God's work; the Word exerts its power without the assistance of man. The church shows itself like a lion in respect to its power of striking terror into its opponents (Isaiah 66:15, 16, 19, 24). It will rend and subdue the nations with the power of the Word. All these facts, described by means of remarkable figures, are now brought out in a statement in the form of a prayerful prediction (v. 9).

42. It will be sufficient to read and briefly summarize this section. Through the church, God strikes the foes (Isaiah 26:11; 54:15, 17). The more the Gospel makes its power felt among the nations, the less will they think of making war and serving idols. God will remove all impediments to the free course of His grace. Note that in this section God is addressing Israel. God's people must not put their confidence in the might of men, the strength of armies, well-fortified cities, and the like (vv. 10–11). The true Israel is not to rely on earthly things, but only on God (Ezekiel 38:11).

All forms of idolatry are to be exterminated (vv. 12–14). Witchcraft and the casting of spells were idolatrous practices, to which the Israelites also often resorted (some Christians still fall for magic, fortune-telling, etc.). They had also erected images of idols, some carved out of wood, others cast from metal, thinking they could combine the worship of the Lord with idol worship. (See Isaiah 2:8, 18–21; 30:22; Zechariah 13:2.) Asherah poles were symbols of the goddess Astarte erected near certain cities. Verse 14 sums up the objects to be exterminated. This points to the purification of the Old Testament church from all idolatry (the Babylonian Captivity cured the Jews of gross idolatry). These verses describe the Messiah's power in turning the hearts of believers away from the vain things of this world to Himself. All who refuse to yield to the power of the Gospel will be consigned to eternal perdition (v. 15).

Lesson 11

Justice and Mercy

Theme verse: *He has showed you, O men, what is good. And what does the* L*ORD require of you? To act justly and to love mercy and to walk humbly with your God.*

Micah 6:8

Objectives

By the power of the Holy Spirit working through God's Word, we will:

- grow in our appreciation of God's rich mercy and forgiveness through Christ;
- become more aware of opportunities for us to provide justice and mercy for the oppressed;
- seek to deal fairly and equally with all people.

In his third address (chapters 6 and 7) Micah points out the way to salvation by showing that the Jews bring punishment upon themselves by their ingratitude and disobedience to God's commandments, but that it is only through sincere repentance that they can avert the judgment they have deserved. This is a most touching chapter in which God is pictured as pleading with His apostate people. A wholly new style is introduced by the prophet to set forth what the true and spiritual religion means. Dramatically the prophet voices the complaint of the Lord, who refuses to be bribed and appeased with meaningless sacrifices and a dead formalism of worship, but who demands true religion of the heart that manifests itself in daily life as godly conduct and charity toward all men. In this chapter Micah portrays some of the great evils we find in our modern life.

43. Note the contrast between verses 1–7 and verse 8, showing on the one hand what the people were like and on the other hand how they should have been. The most remarkable thing about God's dealings

with the Israelites is His boundless mercy and patience. It passes all human understanding why God should at all bother with such stubborn, disobedient, and ungrateful people. But the Scriptures record such examples of God's grace and longsuffering for our instruction and consolation.

Answers may vary.

44. Israel could not deny these "righteous acts" of God. Unable to answer the challenge of the Lord and convicted by its conscience, it looks for a way to make amends. Micah lets the people speak, addressing him as the interpreter of God's will. They are ready to prostrate themselves before the divine Majesty, who is enthroned in heaven (Isaiah 1:11–17; 33:5; Psalm 115:3). They ask, as if they know not, what the Lord requires of them to appease Him. Can they restore their relationship with Him by more and greater sacrifices than those offered regularly at the temple? Note that they make no reference to sin offerings, because they evidence no knowledge and confession of sin. But as burnt offerings they would bring the very best (Leviticus 1): yearling calves (Leviticus 9:2–3); thousands of rams (quantity added to quality); rivers flowing with honey and cream (Job 20:17).

If all this would not be sufficient, then the dearest of all, the first-born son, their very children, they would gladly offer as burnt offerings. They should have known that God detests human sacrifices (Deuteronomy 12:31) such as were common among the heathen (2 Kings 3:27).

Verse 8 shows that such outward offerings were not sufficient to restore the relationship that had been severed. God requires the consecration of the heart and a life dedicated to justice, mercy, and spirituality. Without this dedicated life all sacrifices are vain and empty. Ritual, ceremony, and offerings do not win His favor.

45. True wisdom is the fear and knowledge of the Lord. Such wisdom will accept God's discipline as from a loving Father, who seeks not to condemn, but to correct.

46. Answers may vary.

God opposes all wrongdoing and injustice. His standards for business practices are not lessened because they are "business."

Wealth that is acquired dishonestly brings only guilt and misery. Covetousness is often the cause.

Lesson 12

Pardon and Forgiveness

Theme Verse: *Who is a God like You, who pardons sin and forgives the transgression of the remnant of His inheritance? You do not stay angry forever but delight to show mercy.*

Micah 7:18

Objectives

By the power of the Holy Spirit working through God's Word, we will:

- grow in our knowledge and trust in our gracious God;
- discover the essential difference between Christianity and the world's other religions;
- tell others of God's greatness and love in Christ, the promised Messiah and Savior.

The Book of Micah closes with a glorious climax. The prophet here, as Luther says, gathers together all his prophecies into one bundle, once more condemning the shameful godlessness of his people, but chiefly calling attention to the blessed state of the church under Christ, its Shepherd, and its relationship to the Lord, the great God of all mercy, who forgives all its sin and fulfills all His promises pertaining to its future glory.

47. Answers may vary.

Faith is nowhere kept when justice is perverted (Jeremiah 9:2–6); the most sacred relationships are disregarded. Note how Jesus applies this text to the times of persecution of the New Testament believers (Matthew 10:21, 35–36; Luke 21:16). (See also Matthew 24:10, 12; 2 Timothy 3:1–3.)

The church, taught by chastisement (v. 4) to feel and acknowledge its sin (v. 9), casts itself upon the Lord as its only hope, in patient waiting. "Watch" and "wait"' (v. 7), expresses the believer's faith and hope. "My God" indicates strong, personal faith. The believer is certain that God will answer his prayer (Psalm 27:9; Isaiah 17:10).

48. In all the pagan religions of the world there is not one word about "mercy." Sacrifices, rituals, moral improvements, and other works are prescribed in order to gain or regain favor.

The essential difference between genuine Christianity and all the religions of the world is that the Christian faith is based on God's mercy, His grace through Jesus Christ, and not on human achievement.

We look to Christ and Christ alone for God's mercy and the forgiveness of sins. He is God's promised Son, our Savior, and our Peace (Micah 5:2, 5).